LOUISE NEVELSON
ATMOSPHERES AND ENVIRONMENTS

LOUISE NEVELSON
ATMOSPHERES AND ENVIRONMENTS

INTRODUCTION BY EDWARD ALBEE

Clarkson N. Potter, Inc. / Publishers, New York
DISTRIBUTED BY CROWN PUBLISHERS, INC.
IN ASSOCIATION WITH THE
WHITNEY MUSEUM OF AMERICAN ART, NEW YORK

First published in 1980 by Clarkson N. Potter, Inc.,
One Park Avenue, New York, New York 10016
Printed in the United States of America
Published simultaneously in Canada by General Publishing Company
Limited

Library of Congress Cataloging in Publication Data
Nevelson, Louise, 1899–
Louise Nevelson : atmospheres and environments.
"Published in association with the Whitney Museum of American Art."
Bibliography: p. 172
     1. Nevelson, Louise, 1899–   —Catalogs. I. Albee,
Edward, 1928–   II. Whitney Museum of American Art,
New York.
NB237.N43A4 1980   709'.2'4   79-26221
ISBN: 0-517-540541 (cloth)
          0-517-540517 (paper)

10   9   8   7   6   5   4   3   2   1

Excerpts from *Dawns + Dusks,* taped conversations with Diana MacKown,
are reprinted by permission of Charles Scribner's Sons, copyright © 1976 by
Diana MacKown.

CONTENTS

PREFACE AND ACKNOWLEDGMENTS

I N 1980, THE 50TH ANNIVERSARY of the founding of the Whitney Museum of American Art, we are emphasizing the history and activities of the Museum in many special ways. The most important consideration in all our efforts is the relationship that the Museum has always maintained with artists. This exhibition of the work of Louise Nevelson is an occasion for great pride because it represents both the commitment of the Museum to the artist and that of the artist to the Museum. Nevelson stated in the book *Dawns + Dusks:* "One of the great joys is to know that the Whitney Museum has so much of my work. And I intend to give them more. I love that Museum. First, it is truly *the* American Museum. Secondly, I came in on the ground floor, literally. When the building of the new Whitney was completed in 1967, I had the first retrospective of my work there, so naturally that was very important to me."

About two years ago I suggested to Louise that perhaps in 1980, our anniversary, it might be appropriate to also celebrate an anniversary of hers: her 80th birthday. She agreed, and we did not discuss the matter further. Several weeks later I received a letter expressing her enthusiasm for an exhibition that would confirm once again the central focus of her work: "As you know, my work is usually shown as independent pieces. My personal consideration is for the entire body of work as an atmosphere. I say atmosphere rather than environment because environment has become so nonspecific and my work is so involved with atmospheric mood. As such, I ask that you allow me to design the installation of this exhibition, as I will have very few opportunities to do this again and I would like this to reflect my own projections for my work." It was then decided that we would bring together the components of four separate environments that had been dispersed after their initial presentation plus a fifth environment, *Mrs. N's Palace,* and invite Nevelson to present the core of her creative achievement in one exhibition.

In assembling publications with critical accounts of contemporary artists, we have recently begun to invite people in other disciplines to review the work of visual artists. Louise Nevelson and Edward Albee have been friends for many years and share a respect and admiration for each other's work. Albee's personal association with painters and sculptors makes his contribution to this publication particularly appropriate, and we are indebted to him for giving us new insight into Nevelson and her work.

The illustrations of each of the five environments are preceded by a summary of their history and an iconological interpretation by Laurie Wilson, Assistant Professor at New York University. We asked the photographer Pedro E. Guerrero to attempt to capture Nevelson at this moment of triumph and creativity, and we are sincerely grateful to him for fulfilling the assignment so capably.

Richard Marshall, Associate Curator of the Whitney Museum, has coordinated our efforts with a quiet, forceful hand. In organizing the exhibition, he has collaborated with Nevelson on the selection of works and installation, and coordinated the content of the book. Diana MacKown, Nevelson's assistant, has followed every detail of our work with accuracy and meticulous attention to detail. Nevelson and Arnold Glimcher are models of the liaison between the creative individual and an art dealer. His absolute belief in the artist and her reciprocal trust in him made the planning of the exhibition and the detailed loan arrangements proceed with ease and efficiency.

We would not have been able to present this exhibition without the cooperation of the lenders, both private individuals privileged to live with works of art and public institutions. Schlumberger joins the Whitney Museum for the first time as a corporate sponsor with its support of this exhibition. They have generously applauded the work of the artist and it is an honor to be associated with them on this occasion.

Because of the generosity of Howard and Jean Lipman, the Whitney Museum has the most extensive collection of American sculpture of the past three decades. Nevelson became acquainted with the Lipmans more than twenty-five years ago, and it was their respect for her work and their realization that it should be in a public institution which brought the Whitney Museum and Louise Nevelson together in a lasting relationship. We are at a moment in history when many people who collect works of art are drifting away from any sense of responsibility to artists and public institutions. The work of art has too often become only a means for increasing private worth or self-aggrandizement. Few individuals in our time have dedicated themselves so completely to American art and artists as have Howard and Jean Lipman.

A museum devoted to living artists gains credibility only by balancing the relationship between service to artists and service to the public. This balance can be achieved by maintaining a high standard of quality in exhibition programs as well as in the objects assembled for its collection. In both areas, the Whitney Museum has had a long and close association with Louise Nevelson. In 1956, it was the first museum to purchase a work by Nevelson for its permanent collection. In addition, the Whitney Museum organized her first major museum retrospective in 1967, and held a second exhibition of her work in 1970. The Museum now has more than forty works in all media, representing Nevelson's entire career.

The fact that an artist recognizes the function of a museum and encourages it is very gratifying. For many artists, the intensity of discipline required for their work does not allow their vision to extend beyond its creation. Louise Nevelson understands the role of a public institution in an artist's career. It is an honor to celebrate jointly her anniversary and the anniversary of the Whitney Museum.

TOM ARMSTRONG
Director
Whitney Museum of American Art

LOUISE NEVELSON: ATMOSPHERES AND ENVIRONMENTS

Louise Nevelson: ATMOSPHERES AND ENVIRONMENTS focuses on the seminal period of Nevelson's career when she first used carved, found, and painted wood objects to form entire sculptural walls, and emerged as one of America's leading sculptors. Beginning in the mid-1950s, Nevelson conceived and executed her exhibitions of painted wood constructions as complete environmental installations. Numerous pieces of sculpture were arranged in a gallery space according to an underlying theme—often making cosmic allusions, referring to marriage or to the imaginary travels of exalted personages. Each exhibition was given a single unifying title, and although individual works were independently titled, constructed, and placed, the goal was a single atmospheric installation. These thematic installations were planned to be environmental in the architectural sense and designed so that the sculptures physically surrounded the viewer and often made use of all available space. The installations also created distinct atmospheres that could be perceived, rather than viewed, by the spectator. The vast accumulations of painted wood fragments—boxed, stacked, and hanging—coupled with dramatic lighting and deliberate positioning, created tangible auras of mystery, reverence, and wonderment.

This book, and the exhibition that it accompanies, presents sculptures from the seven major environmental and thematic exhibitions held by Louise Nevelson between 1955 and 1961, and re-presents them as four separate installations. The intent of the exhibition is not to duplicate the contents and placement of the original exhibitions but to closely approximate the mood, theme, and stylistic cohesion of each of the environments. Nevelson has designed the installation of these environments, creating a new environment from numerous sculptures that have not been reassembled since their initial showings over twenty years ago.

The original environments cannot be duplicated since many of the works that comprised them have been lost, destroyed, or, as is Nevelson's practice, incorporated into other works. Nevelson had at first wanted the environments to remain intact. However, when this was not possible, she created smaller, independent sculptures by grouping various boxes and elements together in a new arrangement that often did not correspond to the configuration in the original installation. Included in the following sections are documentary photographs of the original installations and photographs of many independent sculptures from the environments as they now exist.

The first and earliest environment, "The Royal Voyage," is re-created from sculptures exhibited previously in three different exhibitions. Works from "Ancient Games and Ancient Places" (1955), "The Royal Voyage (of the King and Queen of the Sea)" (1956), and "The Forest" (1957), all initially presented at Grand Central Moderns gallery in New York, are brought together, along with newly made pieces, to create a new environment.

"Moon Garden + One," the all-black 1958 exhibition in which Louise Nevelson first introduced the use of stacked boxes that created entire walls of sculpture and sculpture of walls, is re-created here by bringing together many walls and freestanding pieces that originally appeared in that exhibition. Also included are pieces later assembled from elements used in "Moon Garden + One," and pieces which were included in Nevelson's 1959 exhibition, "Sky Columns Presence."

Louise Nevelson's first white environment was "Dawn's Wedding Feast," constructed and installed in 1959. Although this environment was dismantled and eventually dispersed following its only complete showing, most of the pieces from this dazzling celebration in white wood have been reunited on this occasion. "The Royal Tides," the fourth environment presented, was Nevelson's first gold installation and is not based on a thematic narrative as are the previous environments. Many of these gold walls were first shown at the Martha Jackson Gallery, New York, in 1961. Others included in this re-creation of "The Royal Tides" were constructed during the same period and use many similar forms and objects.

Following "The Royal Tides," Nevelson's work became notable for its more uniform construction on a grid format and the predominance of independent pieces of sculpture not associated thematically with an environmental installation. However, the atmospheric and environmental approach continued to be of great interest to Nevelson and was the basis for her installation design of many exhibitions, including her 1967 retrospective exhibition at the Whitney Museum. During the 1970s, Nevelson's environmental concerns were best expressed in large-scale installations done specifically for public spaces. Some recent permanent installations done on a monumental environmental scale for public spaces and private commissions include the all-white interiors for the Chapel of the Good Shepherd at Saint Peter's Church, New York; *Bicentennial Dawn*, created for the lobby of the James A. Byrne Federal Courthouse in Philadelphia; and a grouping of monumental outdoor sculptures for Louise Nevelson Plaza in lower Manhattan.

This book and exhibition culminate with Louise Nevelson's most recent gallery-sized environment. *Mrs. N's Palace* is an actual structure with decorated exterior and interior constructed so that it will remain an independent and lasting environmental sculpture. Its richly decorated walls are accumulations of black-painted wood pieces made by the artist over a fourteen-year period and assembled in 1977 as a permanent realization of her sculptural concerns. *Mrs. N's Palace* is an anthology of ideas, forms, symbols, and moods that the artist has explored for over twenty-five years.

RICHARD MARSHALL
Associate Curator
Whitney Museum of American Art

LOUISE NEVELSON:
THE SUM AND THE PARTS

by Edward Albee

LOUISE NEVELSON has accomplished the age of eighty, unflagged, undiminished as an artist, but with something curiously awry — the fame of her persona overshadows that of her work in the general public mind.

I doubt there are any living American artists photographs of whom elicit more immediate public recognition than Nevelson's. Not even Warhol's retreating, appalled, oddly ghostlike image is more familiar to the casual reader of elegant or lowbrow junk than "the Nevelson" — the foot-long sable eyelashes framing the deep no-nonsense eyes, the coats of many colors, the splendid unexpected jewelry, the profound juxtapositions.

At the same time, I doubt if a majority of the celebrity-conscious who can spot Nevelson in a group party photograph could relate the woman to the work. They may know what Nevelson looks like, but they don't know who she is.

The factors which make celebrities of some living creative artists and which keep others — their equals or better, often as not — in relative shadow are complex. Certainly Hemingway sought the bright lights, the photo essays, the gossip-column mention as a natural (and naturally self-serving) extension of his sense of himself, as naturally as his coevals, Faulkner and Steinbeck, shy men of a private demeanor, found it unnatural. And while history has not yet proved (nor may it, ever) Hemingway a superior writer to the other two, goodness! he is a more famous one.

Examples abound in all the arts. The poet Allen Ginsberg, through his Beat association and his function as a performing poet, is more a public possession than either James Merrill or John Ashbery — though Ashbery seems to be working at putting this to rights.

The composer Ned Rorem, through photographs, volumes of self-exposure, and through his penchant for publishing opinion on almost every subject, is more deeply embedded in the broad public consciousness than either Elliott Carter or George Crumb, two men whose music is doubtless at least the equal of Rorem's.

Warhol — the majority of whose work sells, I suspect, in direct relation to his maintained personal celebrity — is, to my mind's eye, a lesser artist than Jasper Johns or Clyfford Still, say, two whose dedication to the exploitation of their personas is touching in its absence.

But the public possession of the persona of the artist is not necessarily a denigrating sign. Picasso was, for most of his career, a better than first-rate painter, and "that face!" was probably better known than *Les Demoiselles d'Avignon* or *Night Fishing at Antibes.* The ghost of Juan Gris could, however, probably wander into a retrospective of his own work in a public gallery and be asked (politely, to be sure) if he was just browsing or wanted assistance.

Charisma — which is often nothing more than the conscious (or instinctive) desire to exploit the self: commodity as agent — probably misinforms a number of people about absolute values but is a phenomenon which will be with us as long as the public prints realize it is what people want (as opposed to what they should want), and in a consumer-oriented society, especially in a democracy, it can (and should) be no other way.

But what a bizarre picture of the arts — the creative mind — it tolerates, even encourages! I have watched the celebrity of creative artists blossom as their creativity withered, and others go on to do their best work long after the popular consumer thought they had died.

As often as not the public celebration of the creative artist is a combination of

Figure 1
Set for *Tiny Alice* by Edward Albee, 1965 production
Set designed by William Ritman
Photograph © Alix Jeffry

cynical media-exploitation and touchingly naive public homage — albeit to the symbol of the thing (the person) rather than to the thing itself (the work).

And this brings me back to Louise Nevelson, a bird of rare plumage, whose work, at its very best, is as good as any being done in the second half of this century, and whose art and persona are perhaps more the same thing — in the very best of senses — than any other living artist.

My theory is that when we come on this earth, many of us are ready-made. Some of us — most of us — have genes that are ready for certain performances. Nature gives you these gifts. There's no denying that Caruso came with a voice, there's no denying that Beethoven came with music in his soul. Picasso was drawing like an angel in the crib. You're born with it.

I claim for myself I was born this way. From earliest, earliest childhood I knew I was going to be an artist. I felt like an artist. You feel it — just like you feel you're a singer if you have a voice. So I have that blessing, and there was never a time that I questioned it or doubted it.

Some people are here on earth and never knew what they wanted. I call them unfinished business. I had a blueprint all my life from childhood and I knew exactly what I demanded of this world. Now, some people may not demand of life as much as I did. But I wanted one thing that I thought belonged to me. I wanted the whole show. For me, that is living.

I don't say life was easy. For forty years, I wanted to jump out of windows. But I did feel I had the strength and the creative ability. There was never any doubt about that. No one could move me till I got what I wanted — on my terms, on earth. And I do. And it did take, maybe not the greatest mind, but it did take courage. And it did take despair. And the hardship gave me total freedom.

The above — Nevelson speaking of Nevelson — is from an extraordinary book, *Dawns + Dusks* (copyright 1976 by Diana MacKown, published by Charles Scribner's Sons, New York). In part the book is made up of photographs of its subject (Nevelson), the majority of which have been taken by Miss MacKown over the past fifteen or so years, and in part — major part — the book is a result of a transcription of taped conversations between Nevelson and Miss MacKown over a somewhat more recent period of years (1973 – 76).

What emerges is a seamless statement of Nevelson by Nevelson, an almost stream-of-consciousness revelation of that artist's life. It is a major document in the spotty catalogue of art memoirs, and it is accomplished in the very manner in which Nevelson works — *assemblage.*

It is a spoken monologue — that it is written down does not transform it, merely emphasizes the fact — moving with an inevitability (however bewildering from time to time), touching all that has touched Nevelson — the facts of her life, her view of those facts, her progress as a person/artist (/ because in Nevelson's case the two are intertwined in a complexity rare even to the most single-minded creator), seemingly random ruminations on major and minor events, hermetic pronouncements and, now and again, jabs of universal lightning — a catalogue of insights and revelations that displays, not unintentionally I think, guile and candor at work together.

I recommend the book not only to those who admire Nevelson (as an artist and/or personality) but to anyone who desires to gain (however partially) access to the guts of a creative intelligence.

I have referred to this book frequently in preparing this brief essay, most pertinently when I am more interested in Nevelson's view of something Nevelsonian than I am in my own. This is judicious of me, I think, for I am neither art historian nor critic, and

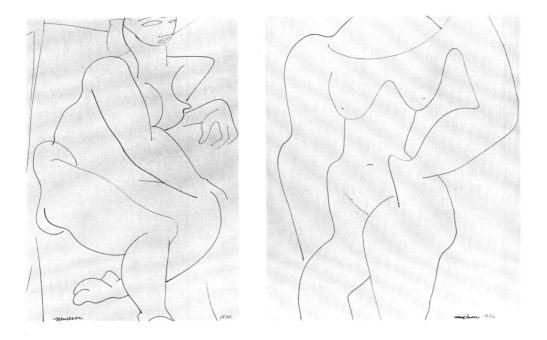

Figures 2, 3
Louise Nevelson
Untitled, 1930
Ink on paper,
20 x 14⅛ inches
Untitled, 1932
Ink on paper,
11¼ x 9 inches
Whitney Museum of
American Art,
New York;
gift of the artist

while I have been asked to give of my response to Nevelson's work for that very reason — to add to the corpus of (occasionally) informed and scholarly essays on the lady's art the view of someone who also practices in the arts — and while my views will not be wholly intuitive (I am as guilty of attempting rational argument as the next writer), I am wise enough to know one or two things about the virtue of the horse's mouth.

Were my response to Nevelson's work not sympathetic — did I not admire greatly a lot of her accomplishment — I would not be writing this introduction, would not have wanted to. At the same time, my reaction to Nevelson's art is doubtless idiosyncratic, and one or two of the conclusions I have come to may startle or dismay either the artist or her champions. Be that as it may, just as Nevelson was one of the few people who saw instinctively to the core of my play *Tiny Alice* (Figure 1), I can bring to bear on my appreciation of her art the whims of my own creative reasoning.

People who practice the arts bring to a discussion of the arts special information unavailable (except as hearsay) to the historian or aesthetician, information — or insight if you will — not necessarily as easily useful to the art-experience recipient as other views may seem but nonetheless often more congruent to the intended relationship of the art to the recipient. And since most art recipients are more interested in how art can be useful to their view of themselves rather than the (I suspect) ultimately more valuable adversary experience in which art is instructive and is an act of aggression against the familiar and the "easy," very few creative artists are hired as critics in the popular and influential media.

But enough of this; on to the matter at hand.

A brief recapitulation of the Louise Nevelson story is in order.

Figure 4
Louise Nevelson
Plaster sculptures, 1932–33
Collection of the artist

In one way this is easy enough to put down on paper, for the outlines of the biography are already available to anyone who wants to read them — dates, events, exhibits, etc. — and there is a chronology elsewhere in this volume which lists such compass markings.

There is a difficulty, though, for facts tell us little, and it is the meaning of facts — what produced them, what they produced — that makes most biography a little less accurate than most autobiography.

Nevelson has said, "I seek truth. What I seek is anything that will work for me; I'll use a lie if it works, and that [becomes] the truth." While Nevelson does not share Blanche DuBois' credo, "I tell what ought to be true" (indeed, I know no person more candid than Nevelson about the implications of facts), she does share the commonly held view among creative artists that facts are less interesting than truth and that, given your lights, you can let a fact lead you into either a pit of darkness or almost blinding illumination.

Example: Nevelson writes that often she was on the verge of suicide (the 1940s, for example). What truth is to be gained from this information? — that Nevelson was psychologically disturbed? or the far more useful and valuable information that Nevelson was frequently in despair during this period because she had not yet been able to release from within herself the art (or view of reality, whichever you like) she knew she contained, was possessed by.

What we make of facts is what we need from them, and the creative mind — which probably has access to the unconscious in ways the noninterpretive does not — understands the purpose of facts in ways we would be unwise not to learn from.

I suppose I could (were I that sort of person) betray the confidence Nevelson has

placed in me as a friend, and speckle this essay with a hundred privileged anecdotes — what she "really" thinks of her contemporaries, what we talk about at a dinner party, what it's "like" to be with her — under the guise of revealing the person (therefore the artist). I *could* do it, and could, through careful selection, reveal Nevelson as saint or devil, but I would not. Friends, doctors, and priests have much the same code, and could I break bread with Nevelson again once having broken her trust?

Besides, except for the very young, creative people don't sit around and discuss aesthetics very much. They discuss themselves — by which I mean they discuss the matters of the world, mundane and otherwise, as seen through the doors of their own perception. This is very interesting to those who share those perceptions, and inexplicable to those who do not.

I have supped with Auden, looked at an ocean with Rothko, drunk wine with Beckett, watched Tennessee Williams swim forty lengths of my pool, gathered wood with Nevelson on the streets of Little Italy. On none of these occasions can I recall a *mot* or a profundity uttered. We were people at ease with one another; there were no reporters about. Yet I could as easily say that I watched "In Praise of Limestone" knife through a steak, for example; was splashed as *Suddenly Last Summer* bellyflopped (no pun intended); or watched an older woman stoop into a Prince Street gutter and come up with a work of art already — not yet, but already — black and inevitable.

The creator and the art are inseparable, once you have known them both.

I hope that I have revealed nothing too heady for the fan or too perplexing to the scholar already wrapped in his theories by having let it slip that Tennessee swims. For the clearest view of Nevelson I point you to her work. She is there.

She is also, I suppose, in the facts of her life. Facts, then.

The artist was born in Kiev, Russia, just before the turn of the century. By 1905 the

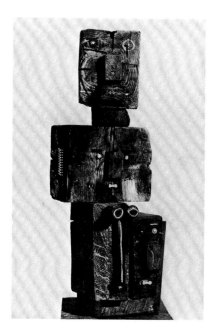

Figures 5, 6, 7
Louise Nevelson
Clown, 1942
Wood and metal, 60 inches
Clown Tightrope Walker, 1942
Wood and metal, 55 inches
Audience Figure, 1942
Painted wood and metal, 60 inches

Destroyed

family (Isaac Berliawsky, his wife, Minna Ziesel, and three children — Nathan, Louise, and Anita) had immigrated to Rockland, Maine, where Louise spent her formative years.

She recalls that she was nine years old when she discovered — to no one's surprise more than her own — that she was going to be an artist.

You know, people always ask children, what are you going to be when you grow up? I remember going to the library, I couldn't have been more than nine. I went with another little girl to get a book. The librarian was a fairly cultivated woman, and she asked my little girl friend, "What are you going to be?" And she said she was going to be a bookkeeper. There was a big plaster Joan of Arc in the center of the library, and I looked at it. Sometimes I would be frightened of things I said because they seemed so automatic. The librarian asked me what I was going to be, and of course I said, "I'm going to be an artist." "No," I added, "I want to be a sculptor, I don't want color to help me." I got so frightened, I ran home crying. How did I know that when I never thought of it before in my life?

Since being an artist is a state of mind, a way of receiving reality and giving it back to the world altered by the artist's perceptions (and improvements?), it is not surprising to us that such a little girl will blurt out her nature, thus discovering it, in such a fashion. What an astonishment to her, though — if not in retrospect.

And it was the beginning of an over-forty-year search for a proper balance between the container (the artist) and the thing contained (the art). Nevelson searched long and far for what she has referred to as "the rudder" and "the grounding," by which she means the moment when the artist and the art fell into harmony and were thus able to assuage one another.

A lot went on between 1908 ("I'm an artist") and the early 1950s, when the harmony finally occurred. Her childhood wasn't exactly happy.

She was a kind of double outsider — a Jewish immigrant in an ASP Yankee town, and also, sensing her own specialness, removed from whatever social and environmental accommodations were to come.

She adored her mother, who was fragile both physically and psychologically, and her feelings toward her father were ambivalent; she admired his intelligence, drive, and resourcefulness, but the two were not close — she found him preoccupied, remote.

This man established himself in lumber (!), and while the family could not be said at that time to have been wealthy, neither did they lack materially. Louise lived the life of many merchant-class young girls: piano lessons, singing lessons, drawing. She was captain of her school basketball team and vice-president of the glee club. And all the while she felt slightly removed from her environment.

You see, you don't choose. From the day you are born there is a pattern, not of your own conscious choosing. I would like to go so far as to say, like an architect of this kind of thinking, that in the future you will claim your true heritage and you will have a choice of taking a name. You will have a choice . . . not having yourself stamped. You will choose. When we're free of this kind of thinking, we'll be free of the other things that surround it.

In retrospect, I think the one thing that kept me going was that I wouldn't be appeased. You know, maybe you see in little children that they're quiet. You give them candy and they're happy. But some of us, even when we were little children, wanted something else — what life really gives. Something that would justify our being here. And I meant it. And I would take nothing less.

Figure 9
Louise Nevelson
Painted wood pieces in
Helena Simkhovitch's garden,
early 1950s

She sensed that she was special, and it was a conviction that stayed with her until finally she proved herself right.

In 1918 a most curious set of events occurred. Louise's father had business dealings with a family from Latvian Russia, a family named Nevelson. There were four brothers; the eldest, Bernard, a married man in his late forties, was introduced to the nineteen-year-old Louise during one of his business visits to Maine. He took a fancy to her, invited her to dinner and, upon his return to New York City, wrote her letters, which she did not answer, fearing that his intentions were dishonorable. (Remember, this was the teens!)

Eventually a letter from Bernard informed Louise that the youngest of the Nevelson brothers — Charles, in his early thirties — was coming to Maine on business in his stead. On the day Charles arrived he telephoned Louise, whom he had never met, inviting her to dinner. She accepted the invitation, hung up, thought for a moment, took her mother into the kitchen and said, "Mr. Charles Nevelson is here, and he's going to propose to me this evening and I'm accepting."

And of course he did, and of course she did.

Was this reckless impetuosity on Louise's part, or was it that she understood the ways of the world intuitively and was making the best of a struck bargain? No matter. All marriages are made somewhere, and those dealt in the boardroom are not necessarily any less successful than love at first sight, nor should the spontaneity — nay, precipitousness — of the girl's decision be any surprise, for she had a developed sense of herself earlier than most young people. What *is* fascinating about this marriage, however, is that the fact of it — the responsibilities, the looming endlessness of its nature, the birth of a son — produced in Louise Nevelson a series of crises so profound

as to wrench the girl into a woman, to throw this woman on a thirty-five-year odyssey toward the self, the odyssey resulting in the work pictured in this book.

Nevelson is more than usually indirect in her public statements about the breakup of her marriage, and I am too good a friend to pry, but overall it appears that marriage was not the rudder, the "something to hold on to" that Nevelson knew she required to make sense out of being alive.

She declined into a severe depression after the birth of her son and, in a sense, ran off in all directions at the same time to raise her spirits and cleanse her psychic palette. She studied voice professionally; she studied acting; she involved herself with metaphysics; she continued her study of painting; she threw herself into the intellectual/creative cauldron of the period. She looked everywhere, hoping to find a mirror. This led her to Munich to study with Hans Hofmann who was, she had been told, "the greatest teacher in the world" at that time.

The experience with Hofmann was profoundly important for Nevelson.

When I went to Europe for the first time, in 1931, I was desperate. I was going through a tough time emotionally, and it broke. Everything broke, and so here I was. It wasn't only art, it was so many psychological problems, motherhood and separation and the struggles within myself. I was caught at that moment in a broken marriage. Everything had collapsed and it was of my own choosing in a way, but that didn't make it easier. On the contrary, it made it harder. I felt myself without rudders, and I felt that I had no terra firma. So I was fighting desperately for a reality. And I went to anything I could think of, including vegetarianism, including all the isms that were available, to try to get a moment of peace. Not as a student — I didn't want to study anything — but out of despair. I had to find something to give me an anchor.

So when I went to Europe that first time, I really began to understand the cube. I had begun to recognize it in the late 1920s, but when I went to Hofmann in 1931 in Germany, I recognized it, I identified it, and it gave me the key to my stability. I had already delved into metaphysics (Krishnamurti) and I found that they had their symbols. Now, according to metaphysics, thinking is circular. The circle is the mechanics of the mind. It is a mind that turns and turns. It doesn't solve anything really. But when you square the circle, you are in the place of wisdom. There you are enlightened. And that's instantaneous. So Cubism already paralleled what I had selected in metaphysics and it gave me law. Not law, legal. I'm talking about order in a visual sense. It gave me definition for the rest of my life about the world. Before that a few years earlier, when I studied at the League, we saw light and shade, but that was nature. We knew that there was a shadow, but we didn't understand, or I didn't, that that shadow was as valid as the light. Just as valid. We wouldn't see light without shadow. We wouldn't see shadow without the light.

So Hofmann taught Cubism: the push and pull. Positive and negative. Cubism gives you a block of space for light. A block of space for shadow. Light and shade are in the universe, but the cube transcends and translates nature into a structure.

I felt that the Cubist movement was one of the greatest awarenesses that the human mind has ever come to.

Nevelson returned to the United States, threw herself even more vigorously into the general intellectual/creative world of New York City and began producing a series of free drawings and anthropomorphic plaster sculptures — the drawings free, lucid, and three-dimensional (Figures 2 and 3), the sculpture most interesting for the private world it suggests. I saw a field of these pieces in Nevelson's studio recently (Figure 4); their sense of themselves — wrong-headed as it occasionally may be — their squat, blunt combination of child's toy and prehistoric monument relates inevitably if indirectly to the mature work of the 1950s and beyond.

Now, it is not my intention to write a biography. It is enough to say that the years from 1932 to 1952 were complex for Nevelson, filled with blind alleys, despairs, searching, discoveries, and constant, quietly accumulated growth, both as a person and an artist.

Nor do I feel the need to intrude upon the academic accomplishments of Arnold Glimcher's book, *Louise Nevelson* (E. P. Dutton and Co., Inc., 1972; reissued 1976). That book catalogues the progress of her work, the exhibits, the critical reaction extensively, and while I do feel that Glimcher (Nevelson's dealer as well as author) protects the artist unnecessarily in his book, sidestepping or glossing over an analysis of the influences of other artists on her development, this may be nothing more than a gentlemanly bow to the artist's view of herself — "Nevelson does not admit to conscious influences, and she does not remember if she even knew the work of Schwitters" (for example).

Notwithstanding, the Glimcher book is comprehensive and, along with Mac-Kown's book, tells us all we can possibly know of Nevelson and her work short of the actual experience of it.

I have mentioned the anthropomorphic pieces of the early 1930s and how I see their connection to the later work (not suggesting, however, that had Nevelson stopped her development with these she would have had her deserved fame).

It is interesting to briefly trace Nevelson's evolution from these pieces through "The Clown Is the Center of His World" show, 1943 (Figures 5, 6, 7), to the work of the Nierendorf Gallery exhibit of 1944 (Figure 8), to two major breakthroughs of the 1950s,

the painted wooden pieces placed in Helena Simkhovitch's garden in the early 1950s (Figure 9) and *First Personage* of 1956 (Plate 13), to the first of the extensive environments, "Moon Garden + One" of 1958.

Unquestionably, there is an extraordinary maturing here, an eventual coming together, through all the influences — ancient and modern, folk and sophisticated, conscious and unconscious — to an ultimate star-burst statement. And it is gratifying that when the breakthrough came, when the art and artist fused, achieved harmony, there were gifted observers ready and eager to applaud. Dorothy Miller, Dore Ashton, Emily Genauer were there to proselytize and push, and, after the death of Nevelson's first real champion, the dealer Karl Nierendorf, another series of women, Lotte Jacobi, Colette Roberts, and Martha Jackson, showed her work at their galleries.

Nevelson has suggested that she is the most feminine of artists.

I feel that my works are definitely feminine. There is something about the feminine mentality that can rise to heaven. The feminine mind is positive and not the same as a man's. I think there is something feminine about the way I work. A man simply couldn't use the means of, say, fingerwork to produce my small pieces. They are like needlework. . . .

My work is delicate; it may look strong, but it is delicate. True strength is delicate. My whole life is in it, and my whole life is feminine, and I work from an entirely different point of view. My work is the creation of a feminine mind — there is no doubt.

And while her reputation rests primarily on the large sculptural pieces and environments pictured in this book, Nevelson herself leans toward her graphics — especially the ones employing lace — as her most personal and even favorite creations (Figure 10).

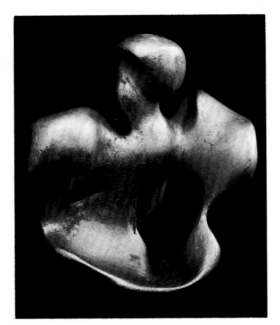

Figure 12
George Vantongerloo
Construction of Volume Relations, 1921
Mahogany, 16⅛ inches high,
4¾ x 4⅛ inches at base
The Museum of Modern Art,
New York; gift of Silvia Pizitz

But the idea of the sex of art troubles me. Certainly the terms cannot apply to the work of Henry Moore and Barbara Hepworth of the 1930s when they were both making brave explorations; and, indeed, Moore's work of the last twenty years can be read as less "masculine" than the gestures Hepworth was making right up to her killing accident. And Anne Ryan was a lesser collagist than Kurt Schwitters, not through any feminine muting of her color sense or any sexually determined structural muddiness, but simply because she was less innovative and had a less compelling creative intelligence.

It is interesting, though, that women have been such a strong force in U.S. art over the past forty years. A couple of valuable books have been appearing lately concerning themselves with first-rate U.S. artists who happen to be women, and I imagine that soon a revealing text about historically important women art dealers of the same period (Betty Parsons, Eleanor Ward, Rose Fried, Edith Halpert, Bertha Schaefer, Martha Jackson, for example) will emerge.

In any event, women of taste and authority were there when Nevelson was ready for them, and if their response to her work was affected by Nevelson's sex, it was, I am certain, unconscious, and it would be the first and only time such a consideration appears in their various judgments as critics and dealers. In fact, I am inclined to dismiss the suggestion as nonsense.

If Nevelson's art is feminine it is not a public matter, and certainly it was no whiff of musk that made Hilton Kramer one of Nevelson's strongest champions; it was merely his alert mind, sharp eye, and generosity of spirit. In his comments on Nevelson's *Sky Cathedrals*, published in *Arts* (June 1958), he writes:

Figure 13
Joaquin Torres Garcia
Superimposed Forms in Color, 1931
Painted wood, 14¼ x 11 inches
Property of Torres Garcia family

They are appalling and marvelous; utterly shocking in the way they violate our received ideas on the limits of sculpture and on the confusion of genres, yet profoundly exhilarating in the way they open an entire realm of possibility. They follow the lead of current abstract painting in projecting an image so large that the spectator is invited to feel "placed" (or trapped perhaps?) within it. For myself, I think Mrs. Nevelson succeeds where the painters often fail. Where they have progressively emptied their image in order to enlarge it, she insists on proliferating more and more detail, arresting the eye with a brilliant or subtle "passage" wherever its glance falls. Where her contemporaries err on the side of frugality and emptiness, she has moved swiftly into a kind of gluttony of images. The results are sometimes ungainly but still overwhelming in force, and what redeems the ungainliness is the exactitude which sustains her hand even at the outer reaches of extravagance. The *Sky Cathedrals* seem to promise something entirely new in the realm of architectural sculpture by turning the tables (or the *walls* perhaps?) on the architects and postulating a sculptural architecture. Whether the austerity and sterility of contemporary architectural practice can take up this challenge remains to be seen. In the realm of sculpture, anyway, the achievement is already there.

Biography, as I said, is not my intention, and I have made concentrated reference to the first thirty years or so of Nevelson's world merely to lay the groundwork for my feelings. An understanding of Nevelson's oeuvre is possible only when one comprehends that what she has been attempting all along is something other than works of art, as the term is commonly understood. Oh, she has been creating works of art all along, individual and collective assemblages, but from the middle 1950s all of Nevelson's work (all her pieces) has been one enormous sculptural idea — or world, if you will.

This is not to suggest that the "parts" are any less interesting than the "sum." Indeed, on many occasions the reasoning is easily as interesting as the conclusion — to me, at any rate — for it can be a kind of miniature course in twentieth-century art history, a view of the sources which lead to the highly original result.

A word here is in order to clear up the quote in Arnold Glimcher's book — "Nevelson does not admit to conscious influences."

The truth, of course, is that Nevelson is neither a self-conscious primitive nor a fool; she knows that she, along with almost every other valuable artist, has been influenced by everything that she has seen, heard, touched. It is merely that her mind absorbs stimuli for later use without making a conscious checklist of the materials filed away. All matter we absorb is either nutriment or waste, and we treat it accordingly.

Did Nevelson's interests in African, Aztec, and Mayan art, folk weaving — fabrics of all kinds, in fact — affect her work? Of course; sometimes directly (certainly neither more nor less than Picasso's first exposure to African sculpture "blew his mind," as they say these days) and sometimes only to the extent of broadening — ordering — her perceptions.

And what do we say of the family resemblances between individual statements by Nevelson and certain pieces by Schwitters, Picasso (Figure 11), Vantongerloo (Figure 12), Tatlin, and even Torres Garcia (Figure 13)? Did Nevelson know these works? Was she consciously influenced by them? Does it matter? If we are not influenced (directly or indirectly) by a specific important art statement, the chances are very great that we *have* been influenced either by its precedents or successors.

The very best of Nevelson's individual assemblages, or structures, or sculptures (or drawings, as she has referred to them) are, variously, exquisite, powerful, remote, primordial, and always intellectually stimulating. They do things to the mind akin to what a Bach two- or three-part invention does.

But it is when these singularities are combined, joined in company to many

Figures 14, 15
Kurt Schwitters
The Hanover Merzbau, begun 1920
Destroyed

others — assemblage of assemblage — that they accumulate an emotional intensity that is the essence of Nevelson's specialness.

Let me take *Mrs. N's Palace* as a case in point. Of all the structures pictured in this volume, it is the only one which can swallow us up in the actual experience of it. With the others — "Dawn's Wedding Feast" or "The Royal Voyage," for example — one can be surrounded, one can move through or past, but the *Palace* is the only one through which one literally enters Nevelson's world, is engulfed by it.

My first experience of this piece (or work) was emotionally as well as intellectually involving — intensely so on both levels. I had a similar experience a few years earlier; I sat in the reconstruction of a room Mondrian had designed; imagine a Mondrian painting twenty by twenty feet; then imagine it a cube; then imagine yourself placed in the center of the cube. On both occasions — the Mondrian and the Nevelson — I had been transformed from spectator to participant. I suspect Schwitters' *Merzbau* (Figures 14, 15), and Kiesler's *The Endless House* (Figure 16), would have been related experiences.

Nevelson tells me that she is a trifle bothered by *Mrs. N's Palace* because it is the only one of the large environments which is made up of pieces made at many different periods of time (1964–77). All of the others ("The Royal Voyage," 1956, for example) are, at least in theory, of a stylistic unity, but it is this very catalogue of Nevelsonia that is *Mrs. N's Palace* that makes it for me not only an enriching and stimulating experience but a touching one as well. When I enter that piece, when I walk around it, when I examine the (how many!?) individual elements, I have the sense of being in the presence of the complete Nevelson. To mangle the Bach simile (but I don't care) — in

Figure 16
Frederick Kiesler
The Endless House, 1959–61
Cement and wire-mesh model,
38 x 42 x 26 inches
André Emmerich Gallery Inc., New York

the presence of so many of the inventions I am also in the presence of one of the great fugues.

Nevelson feels that she began making her "worlds" as an alternative space, so to speak — to create for herself a fathomable reality in the midst of the outside chaos. What has happened, of course, is that the private has become public, the refuge accessible to all, and, to those who know what a Nevelson looks like, the world is beginning to resemble her art.

I hope she's pleased.

THE ARTIST IN HER ENVIRONMENT

PHOTOGRAPHS BY PEDRO E. GUERRERO

THE ROYAL VOYAGE

overleaf

THE ROYAL VOYAGE (OF THE KING AND QUEEN OF THE SEA)
Grand Central Moderns, New York
February 18 – March 8, 1956

Different people have different memories. Some have memories for words, some for action — mine happens to be for form. Basically, my memory is for wood, which gives a certain kind of form — it isn't too hard and it isn't too soft.

I just automatically went to wood. I wanted a medium that was immediate. Wood was the thing that I could communicate with almost spontaneously and get what I was looking for. For me, I think it's the textures and the livingness. . . . When I'm working with wood, it's very alive. It has a life of its own. If this wood wasn't alive, it would be dust. It would disintegrate to nothing. The fact that it's wood means it has another life.

Of course we have lived with wood through the ages: the furniture in the house, the floors of the house. There was a time before cement when the sidewalks were made of wood. Maybe my eye has a great memory of many centuries. And maybe there's something about wood that is closer to the feminine, too.

ANCIENT GAMES AND ANCIENT PLACES (1955) was Louise Nevelson's first one-woman show of sculpture in a decade. A piece entitled *Bride of the Black Moon* was the central figure in this exhibition; it was surrounded by four black-stained wood pieces representing the four continents visited by the bride: *Black Majesty, Forgotten City, Night Scapes,* and *Cloud City.*

These landscapes were derived from a series of cityscapes on which Nevelson had been working for about a year. Inspired by the silhouette of New York City, she began to align found wood fragments along a horizontal plane. Soon these pieces were extended in both height and breadth, and the number of elements in the individual works increased. *Moon Spikes, Black Horizontal, East River City Scape,* and *Black Majesty* represent this development. In *Black Majesty,* we see the parade of vertical elements along a horizontal format being used to suggest figures. In making all of these works, Nevelson had used the scrap wood found at her local lumberyards, pieces of furniture, decorative house ornaments, and whatever interestingly shaped wood objects she and her friends could scavenge from the streets of the city.

Figures predominate in "The Royal Voyage," her exhibition the following year. The most imposing are the *King* and *Queen of the Sea,* two large totemic wood planks that towered over the other works in the show. These black-stained wood figures had traveled to distant lands where they found another *Forgotten City* and some undersea kingdoms, *Undermarine Scape.* On the voyage they were accompanied by a *Chief,* whose spiked angular protrusions hint at his American Indian origins. This show also marks the beginning of Nevelson's uniform use of black for sculpture.

In 1957, in Nevelson's next thematically titled exhibition, "The Forest," the scene shifts to the territory of her youth in Rockland, Maine. A number of seascapes and images representing various aspects of the forest were placed in a broad circle around a group of pieces portraying the village. *Pink Leaf* was one of the large wood pieces in this show which the artist had carved and filed. The delicately incised lines on its surface are reminiscent of both her series of etchings done at Atelier 17 (1953–55), a well-known graphics workshop in New York, and of the terra-cotta pieces done in the early fifties that immediately preceded her return to work in wood. The meandering lines she had used in those two media now roughly approximate the veined surface of the leaf.

The largest work in "The Forest" was another carved piece, *First Personage*. In this remarkable sculpture, the viewer is confronted with a huge slab of wood whose subtly shaped outline suggests a human presence. This frontal plank presents a quiet exterior of repose. But from behind appear the jagged edges of a spiked pole. The artist has referred to *First Personage* as a bride, and initially she had prepared two pieces representing the wedding motif for inclusion in this exhibition.[1] They were originally titled *Wedding Cake* and *Wedding Bridge.* Characteristically, Nevelson changed the composition of the exhibition at the last moment and excluded these two works from the show. This is the last work that Nevelson has carved and, in fact, one of the last designed to be seen in the round. Seeking a more private and hermetic style, she began at the time of this show to enclose her work in boxes.

"The Forest" marked a turning point. The enthusiastic critical response, particularly by Hilton Kramer and Dore Ashton, foretold the sensational success to come.

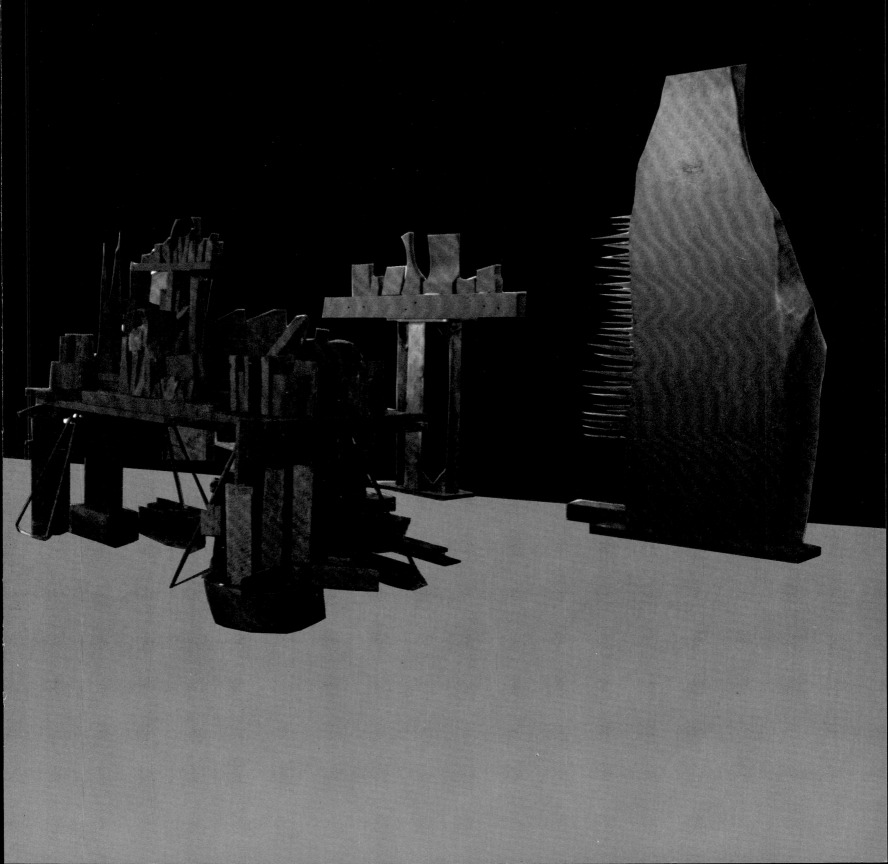

1 *Moon Spikes,* ca. 1953
Wood painted black, 17 x 54 x 9 inches
The Pace Gallery, New York

2 Black Majesty, 1955
Wood painted black, 28 x 32 x 19 inches
Whitney Museum of American Art, New York;
gift of Mr. and Mrs. Ben Mildwoff through the
Federation of Modern Painters and Sculptors, Inc.

3 *The Wave*, 1958
Wood painted black, 28 x 21½ x 10½ inches
The Pace Gallery, New York

4 *Undermarine Scape*, 1956
Wood painted black, glass, and metal,
28½ x 17½ x 17 inches
Ben Mildwoff, New York

5 Black Wedding Cake, ca. 1957
Wood painted black, 38½ inches high
x 24 inches diameter
Dorothy H. Rautbord, Palm Beach, Florida

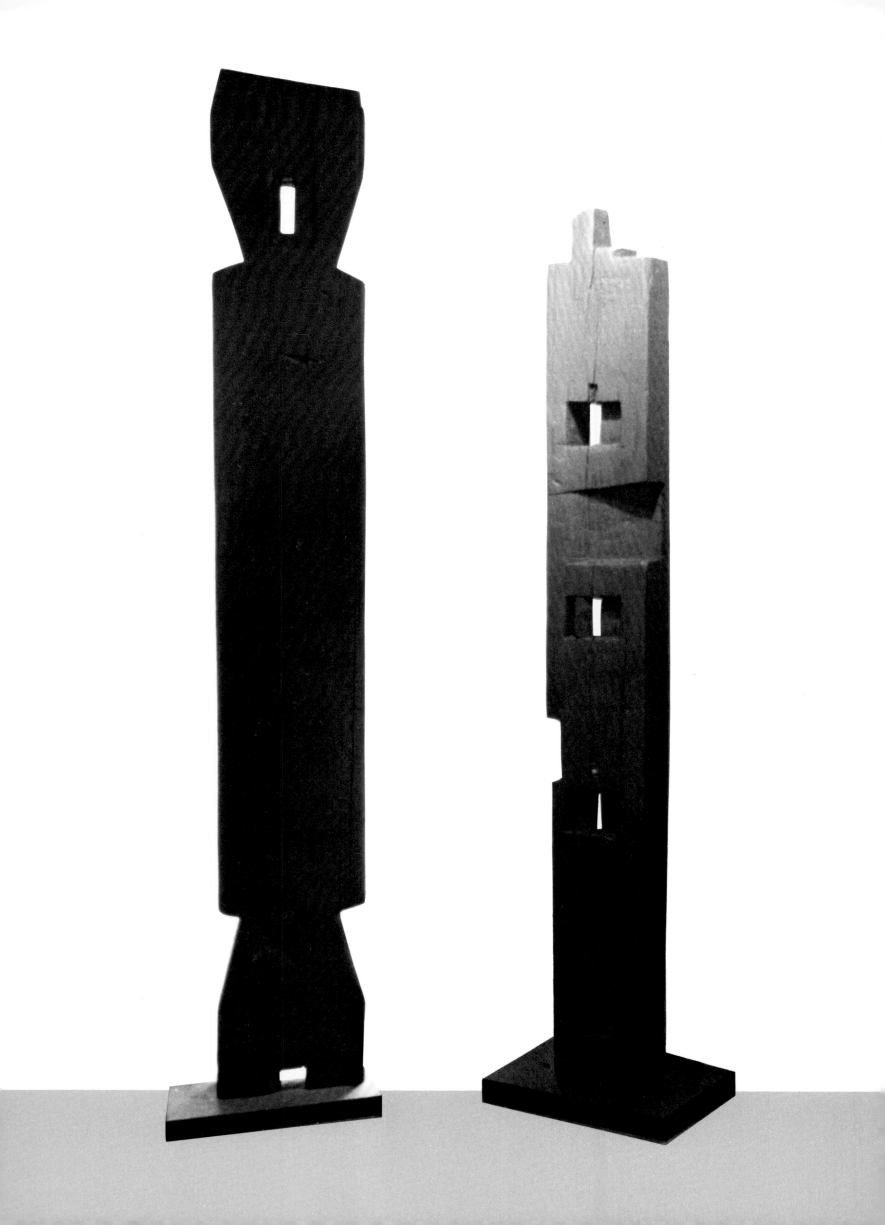

6 *King*, 1956
Wood painted black, approximately
96 x 24 x 12 inches
Destroyed

7 *Queen*, 1956
Wood painted black, approximately
84 x 20 x 8 inches Destroyed

8 *Forgotten City*, 1955
Wood painted black, 85¾ x 30¾ x 11¼ inches
Grey Art Gallery and Study Center,
New York University Art Collection;
gift of Mrs. Anita Berliawsky

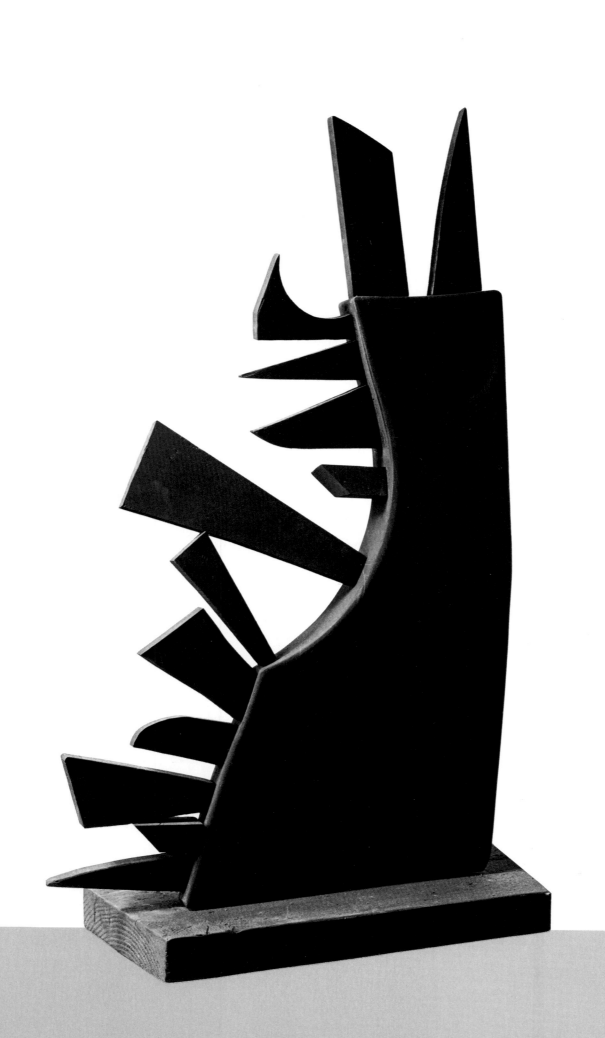

9 *Chief,* 1955
Wood painted black, 48 x 27 x 8¾ inches
Barrett N. Linde, Washington, D.C.

10 *Pink Leaf,* 1956
Wood painted black, 27½ x 46 x 7 inches
Museum of Art, Carnegie Institute, Pittsburgh

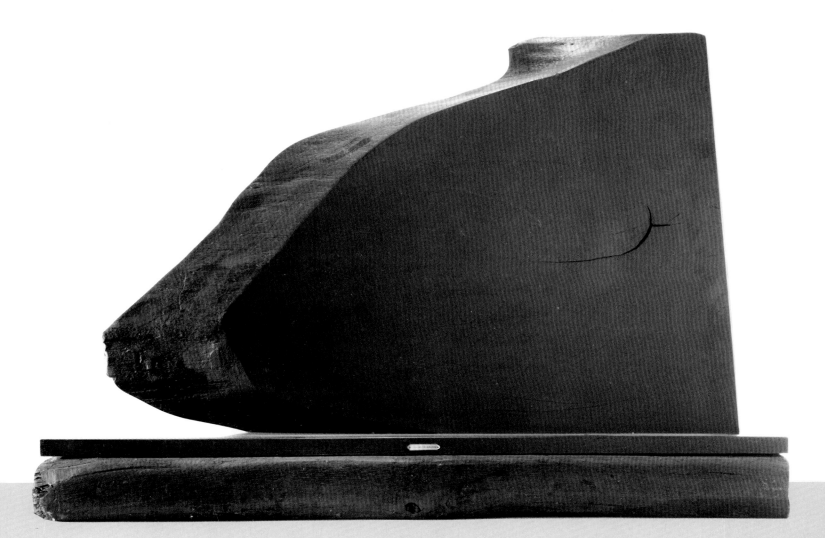

11 *East River City Scape,* 1956
Wood painted black, 23 x 30½ x 16 inches
Weatherspoon Art Gallery, University of
North Carolina at Greensboro

12 *Night Presence VI*, 1955
Wood painted black, 11 x 33 x 8½ inches
Mrs. Vivian Merrin, New York

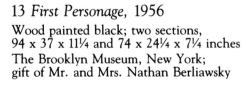

13 *First Personage*, 1956
Wood painted black; two sections,
94 x 37 x 11¼ and 74 x 24¼ x 7¼ inches
The Brooklyn Museum, New York;
gift of Mr. and Mrs. Nathan Berliawsky

MOON GARDEN + ONE

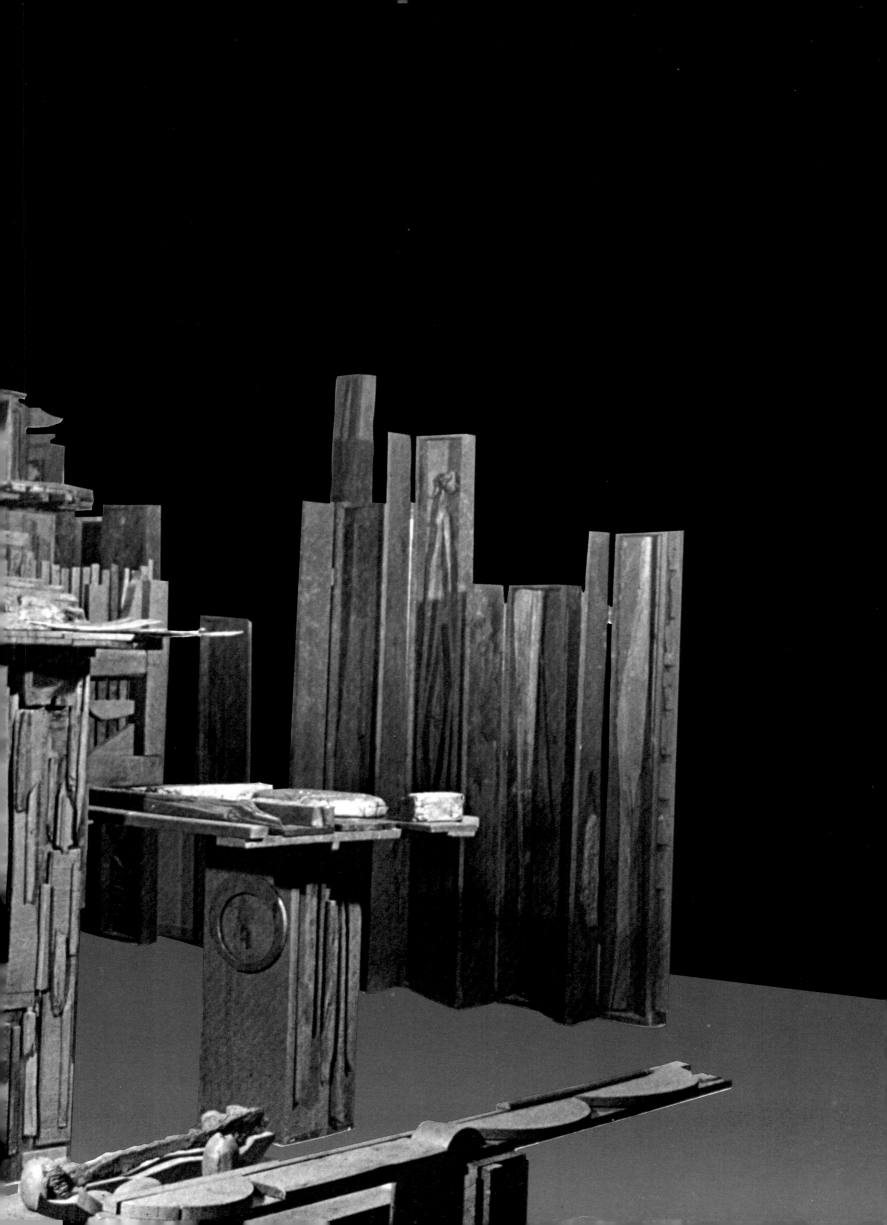

I attribute the walls to this: I had loads of energy. I mean, energy and energy and loads of creative energy. And no matter how much space — now it's different — but at that time if I'd had a city block it wouldn't have been enough because I had this energy that was flowing like an ocean into creativity. Now I think a brook is beautiful and a lake you can look at and it's just peaceful and glorious, but I identify with the ocean. So I began to stack my sculptures into an environment. It was natural. It was a flowing of energy.

I think there is something in the consciousness of the creative person that adds up, and the multiple image that I give, say, in an enormous wall gives me so much satisfaction. There is great satisfaction in seeing a splendid, big, enormous work of art. I'm fully aware that the small object can be very precious and very important. But to me personally, there is something in size and scale.

MOON GARDEN + ONE opened in January 1958 and was greeted with astonishment and enthusiasm by the New York art world. One wall of the Grand Central Moderns gallery was covered by Nevelson's first sculptural wall of black boxes, *Sky Cathedral.* Various groupings of vertical boxes, such as *Black Mirror II* and *King II,* lined other gallery walls like ominous specters. With the exception of some centrally placed pieces on pedestals—*Moon Dial, Moon Fountain,* and *Heavenly Gate*— almost all the works in this exhibition were boxes, doorless or with hinged doors. A few blue lights illuminated the whole show, and in the dimness of the gallery, Nevelson's black boxes were shrouded with an air of mystery. Such darkly dramatic and enveloping effects caused a sensation, and the exhibition was immediately hailed as a disquieting world of fantasy—"A dark place of dreams and loneliness."[2]

Following this critical success, Nevelson was occupied in 1958 with moving to a new home on Spring Street, changing galleries from Grand Central Moderns to the Martha Jackson Gallery, and continuing with her work. During the year, parts of "Moon Garden + One" were reassembled as walls and titled *Tropical Garden I* and *II.* In 1959, she prepared for two major shows simultaneously—"Sky Columns Presence" and "Dawn's Wedding Feast," which were to be held in November and December.

"Sky Columns Presence," at the Martha Jackson Gallery, was a black show. In the spirit of "Moon Garden + One," a gallery wall was completely lined with black boxes. Along the other walls were groups of tall columnar reliefs. Nine years before, Nevelson had made two trips to see Mayan ruins in the Yucatan peninsula of Central America. The striking visual similarities between the artist's four-sided columns covered with low relief and the monumental stelae at the pre-Columbian sites suggest the importance of this ancient art for Nevelson. We can even find the two principal Mayan deities in the enclosed relief tondos entitled *Sun* and *Moon* which stood in the center of the exhibition.

Unlike the blue lighting of "Moon Garden + One," the lighting of "Sky Columns Presence" was designed by Schuyler Watts to promote a unified and enigmatic atmosphere.[3] Originally, Nevelson wanted no lights for "Moon Garden + One," but several hours before the opening decided to use a small amount of colored light. Once the lighting and final placement of the pieces in "Moon Garden + One" were determined, Nevelson and Ted Hazeltine, a former dancer and her devoted young assistant, spontaneously celebrated the completion of this innovative environment by doing a ritual dance in front of the installation.[4]

SKY COLUMNS PRESENCE
Martha Jackson Gallery, New York
October 28 – November 21, 1959

14 *Bouquet (World Garden II)*, 1957
Wood painted black, 54 x 14 x 14 inches
Mark Le Jeune, Kapellenbos, Belgium

15 *Moon Fountain*, 1957
Wood painted black, 43 x 36½ x 34 inches
The Pace Gallery, New York

16 *Black Mirror II*, 1957
Wood painted black, 72 x 8¾ x 5¾ inches
Martha Jackson Gallery, Inc., New York

17 *Untitled*, 1959
Wood painted black, 49 x 21¼ x 10½ inches
Private collection

18 *Sky Cathedral Presence*, 1951–64
Wood painted black, 117 x 200 x 23 inches
Walker Art Center, Minneapolis;
gift of Mr. and Mrs. Kenneth N. Dayton

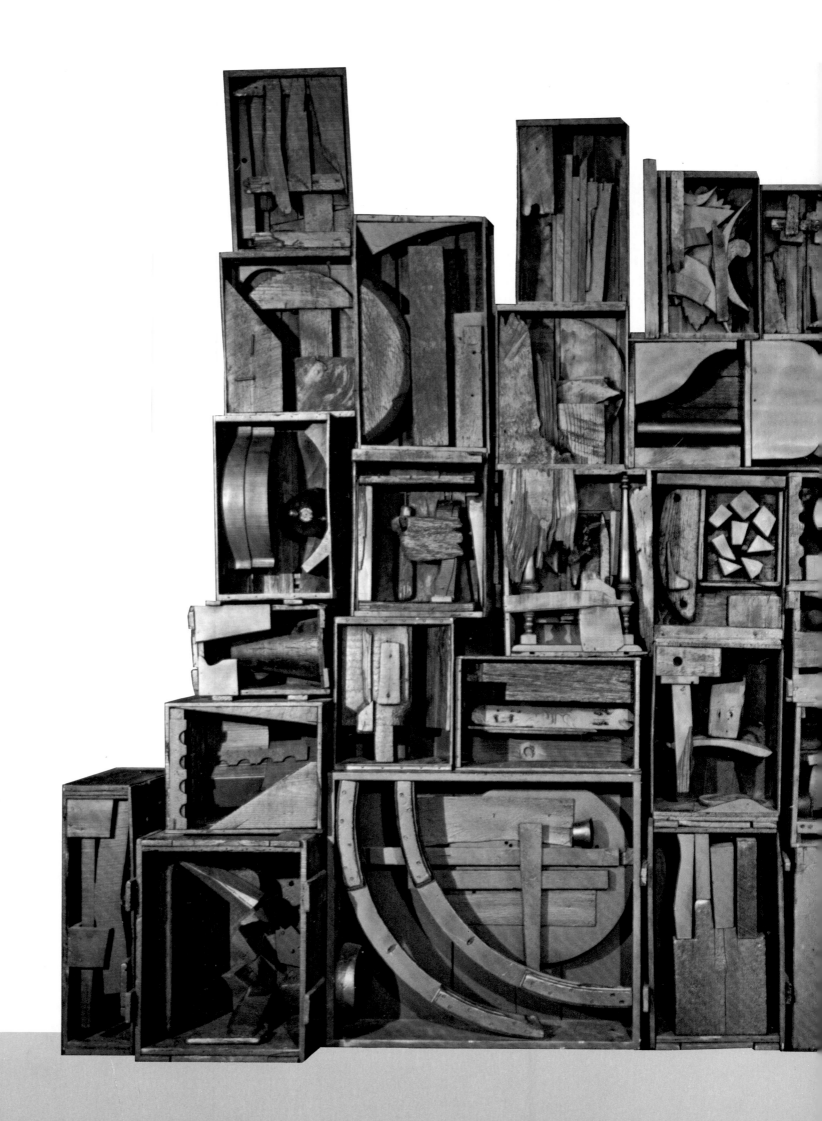

19 *Sky Cathedral*, 1958
Wood painted black, 102½ x 133½ x 20 inches
Albright-Knox Art Gallery, Buffalo, New York;
George B. and Jenny R. Mathews Fund, 1970

20 Tropical Garden II, 1957–59
Wood painted black, 71½ x 131¾ x 12 inches
Musée National d'Art Moderne,
Centre Georges Pompidou, Paris

21 *Young Shadows*, 1959–60
Wood painted black, 114 x 126 x 7¾ inches
Whitney Museum of American Art, New York;
gift of the Friends of the Whitney Museum of
American Art and Charles Simon

22 *Moon Garden Reflections*, ca. 1957
Wood painted black, 72 x 30 x 10 inches
Mr. and Mrs. Burton Tremaine,
Meriden, Connecticut

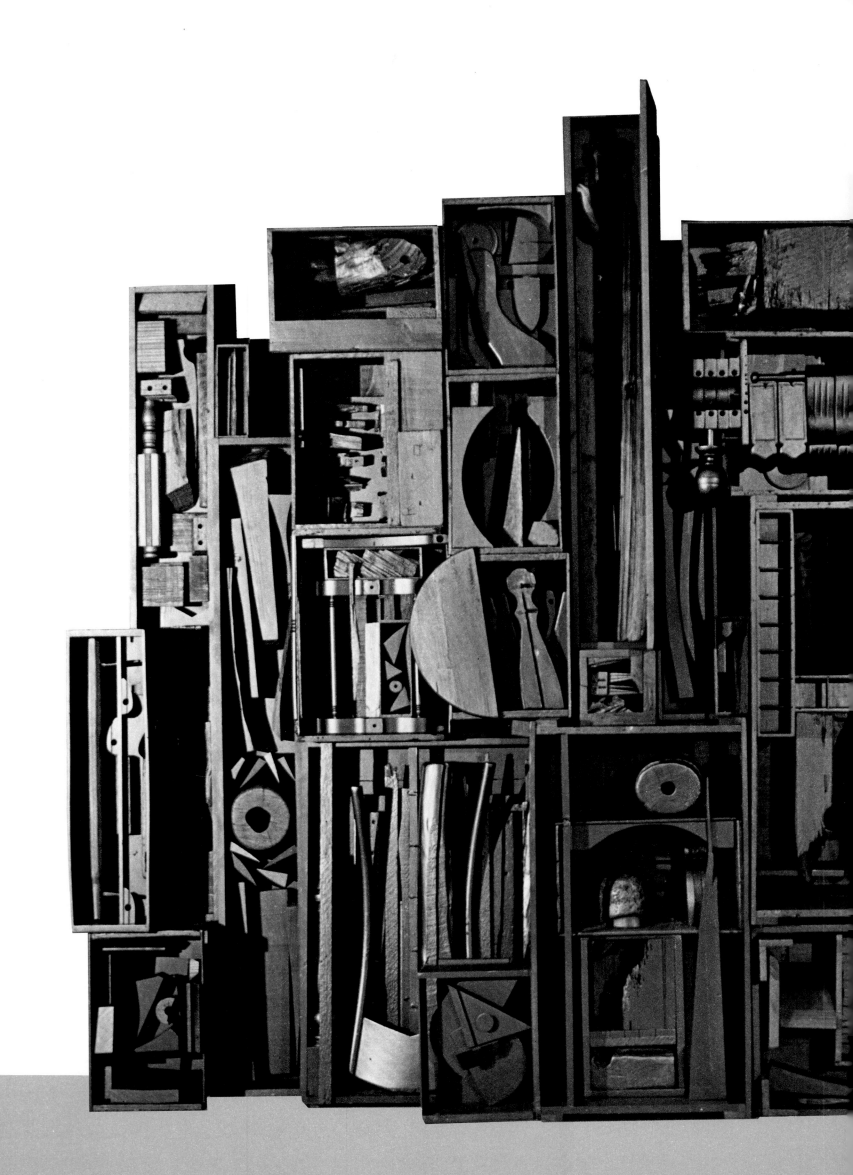

23 Sky Cathedral—Moon Garden + One, 1957–60
Wood painted black, 109 x 130 x 19 inches
Milly and Arnold Glimcher, New York

24 *Sky Cathedral—Moon Garden Wall,* 1956–59
Wood painted black, 85⅝ x 75¼ x 12⅛ inches
The Cleveland Museum of Art;
gift of the Mildred Andrews Fund

25 *Sky Cathedral,* 1958
Wood painted black, 135½ x 102¼ x 18 inches
The Museum of Modern Art, New York;
gift of Mr. and Mrs. Ben Mildwoff

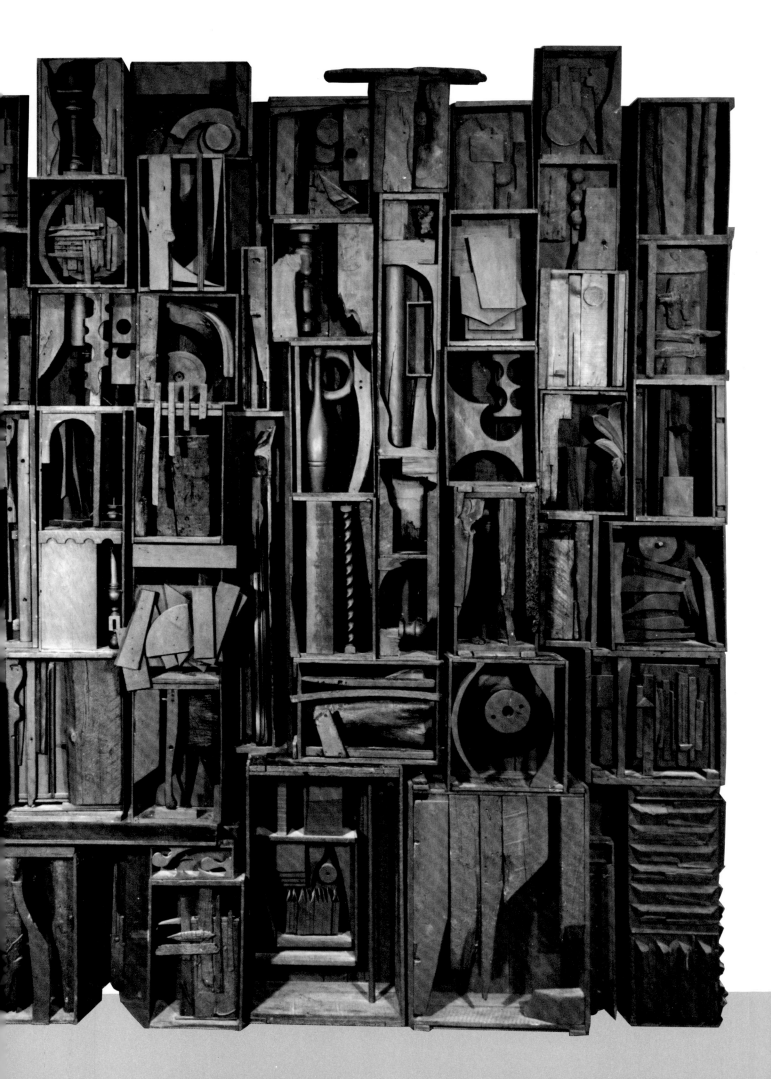

26 *Black Moon*, 1959
Wood painted black, 81 x 30 x 18 inches
Martha Jackson Gallery, Inc., New York

27 *Black Sun*, 1959
Wood painted black, 30 x 24 x 10 inches
Mrs. H. Gates Lloyd, Haverford, Pennsylvania

DAWN'S WEDDING FEAST

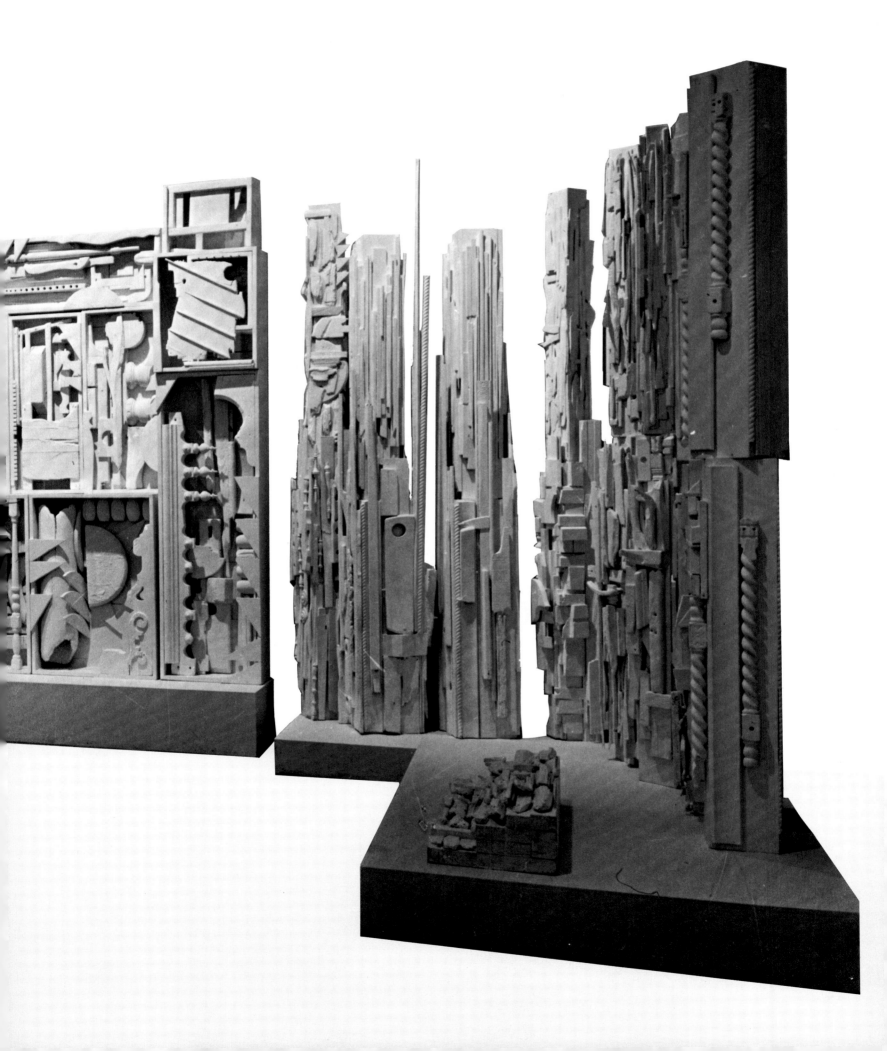

overleaf

DAWN'S WEDDING FEAST
The Museum of Modern Art, New York
December 16, 1959 – February 14, 1960

It is early morning when you arise between night and dawn. When you've slept and the city has slept, you get a psychic vision of an awakening. And between the dream and the awakening, it is celestial. White invites more activity. Because the world is a little bit asleep and you are basically more alive to what's coming through the day.

If you paint a thing black or you paint a thing white, it takes on a whole different dimension. The white and the black invite different forms. A state of mind enters into it. Forms have to speak, and color—this is what has happened to visual art. Now white is what was in my mind. I feel that the white permits a little something to enter. I don't know whether it's a mood. Just as you see it in the universe. The white is more festive. The forms have just that edge. For me, the black contains the silhouette, the essence of the universe. But the whites move out a little bit into outer space with more freedom.

IN 1959, Dorothy Miller, Nevelson's friend of many years and curator at The Museum of Modern Art, offered the artist an opportunity to participate in "Sixteen Americans," one of a series of exhibitions at the museum devoted to American artists. Nevelson accepted immediately and proposed a white environment — "Dawn's Wedding Feast" — her first nonblack show in five years.

Working simultaneously on "Sky Columns Presence" and "Dawn's Wedding Feast," Nevelson rented a separate studio to prepare the white work and to keep it a secret until the opening. The dazzling splendor of this show was, as Nevelson has said: "A wish fulfillment, a transition to a marriage with the world."[5] The largest room was allotted to her and she placed a 16-foot-long wall of boxes called *Dawn's Wedding Chapel* against most of the back wall. Embedded in the center of this section was *Dawn's Wedding Mirror,* a box enclosing a composition organized by a large oval frame encircling a toilet seat cover. To the right of the wall of boxes were two platforms forming an L against the back and side walls. Groups of tall, thin, encrusted columns stood near the wall on each platform. In front of one group lay a steplike set of boxes — *Dawn's Wedding Pillow.* A pair of large two-piece columns stood in the center of the room on a platform opposite the *Wedding Chapel* wall. Several hanging columns, a disk, and a few more boxes made up the remainder of the exhibition.

Two years later, many of the works from this show appeared in one of the three rooms Nevelson was given at the 1962 Venice Biennale. Here, too, she created a white environment, but titled the room *Voyage.* Eventually, despite the artist's hope that this environment might be preserved intact, the very large original wedding chapel was divided into a number of smaller sections and sold to separate collectors.

The persistent occurrence of the wedding theme in Nevelson's work suggests its importance for the artist. The first bride figure to appear was a composition stone piece of 1952 called *Bride of the Sea.* The next was *Bride of the Black Moon* from "Ancient Games and Ancient Places," and that was soon followed by *First Personage,* the work portraying the bride in "The Forest."

"Dawn's Wedding Feast" was the first exhibition devoted entirely to the bride and the wedding theme. Here one would expect to find a work actually representing the bride, but the few titled pieces in the show do not locate her. The central figures are the two large totemic columns on the platform in front of the *Wedding Chapel* wall. The columns are unmistakably figurative, with their larger lower sections and their heavily encrusted narrow upper parts. To each column is attached a round shield bearing a low relief. On one of the shields, the relief elements are emphatically vertical. The tondo on the other column bore three square frames, each enclosing a delicate relief.

These two shields are similar to the *Sun* and *Moon* pieces from "Sky Columns Presence." The differences in the design of both sets not only indicate the different solar bodies, but also suggest differences of gender. Thus the black *Moon* has wood fragments that appear like a woman's hair surrounding a faceted circular face. As with the two columns in "Dawn's Wedding Feast," the *Sun* and *Moon* pieces were placed in the center of the room as focal points in the exhibition. The two large columns in "Dawn's Wedding Feast," carrying perhaps the respective shields of sun and moon, appear to be the feted couple in whose honor the other columnal figures have gathered at the chapel. Thus, the bride, radiant like the dawn and robed in shimmering white, greets the world.

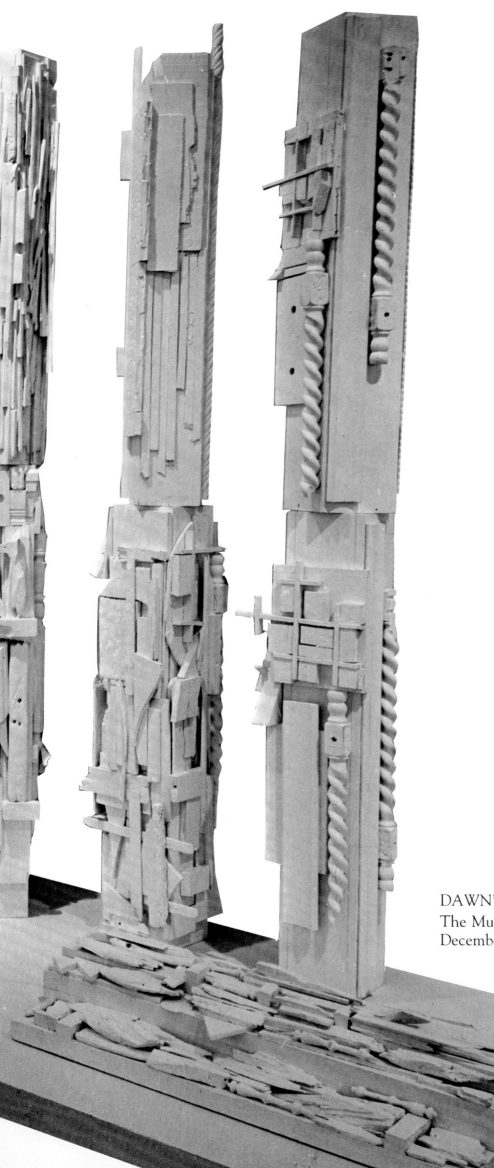

DAWN'S WEDDING FEAST
The Museum of Modern Art, New York
December 16, 1959 – February 14, 1960

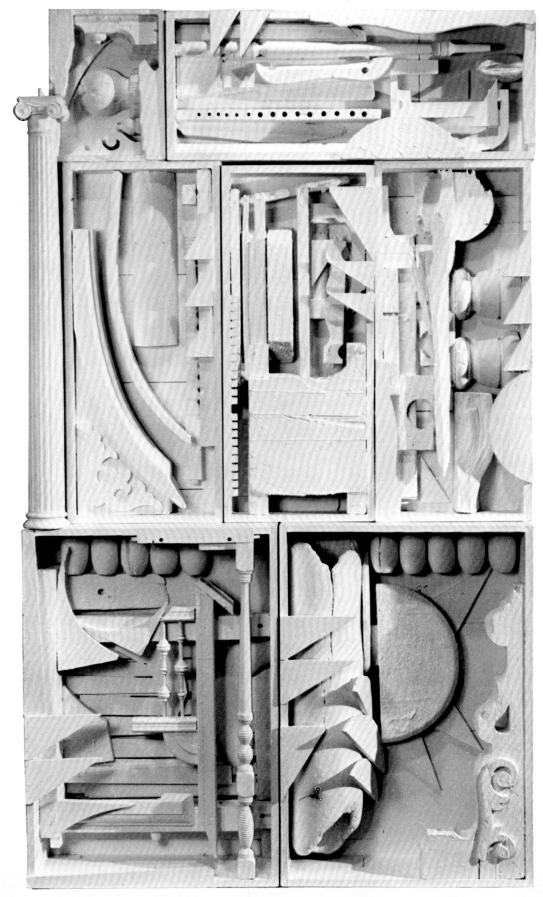

28 *Dawn's Wedding Chapel I,* 1959
Wood painted white, 90 x 51 x 6 inches
Dr. John W. Horton, Cupertino, California

29 *Dawn's Wedding Chapel II,* 1959
Wood painted white,
115⅞ x 83½ x 10½ inches
Whitney Museum of American Art,
New York; gift of the Howard and
Jean Lipman Foundation, Inc.

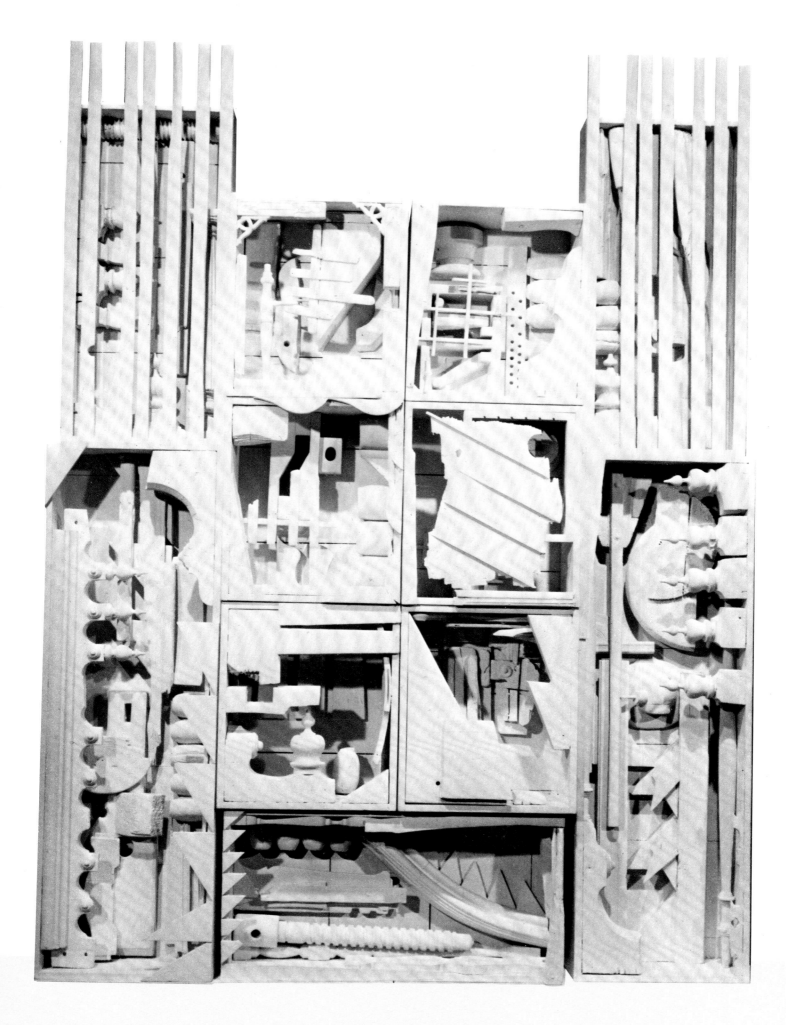

30 *Dawn's Wedding Mirror,* 1959
Wood painted white, 26½ x 31 x 7½ inches
Dr. John W. Horton, Cupertino, California

31 *Dawn's Wedding Cake*, 1959
Wood painted white, approximately 20 inches
high x 36 inches diameter
Destroyed

32 *Dawn's Wedding Chest*, 1959
Wood painted white, 27 x 15 x 6 inches
Mr. and Mrs. Alvin S. Lane, New York

33 *Dawn's Wedding Pillow*, 1959
Wood painted white, 6½ x 36 x 13 inches
Dr. John W. Horton, Cupertino, California

34 *Dawn Column II*, 1959
Wood painted white, 97 x 8½ x 7½ inches
Martha Jackson Gallery, Inc., New York

35 *Dawn Column V*, 1959–60
Wood painted white, 98 x 8 x 7½ inches
Martha Jackson Gallery, Inc., New York

36 *Dawn Lake*, 1959
Wood painted white, 68¼ x 41½ x 4 inches
Martha Jackson Gallery, Inc., New York

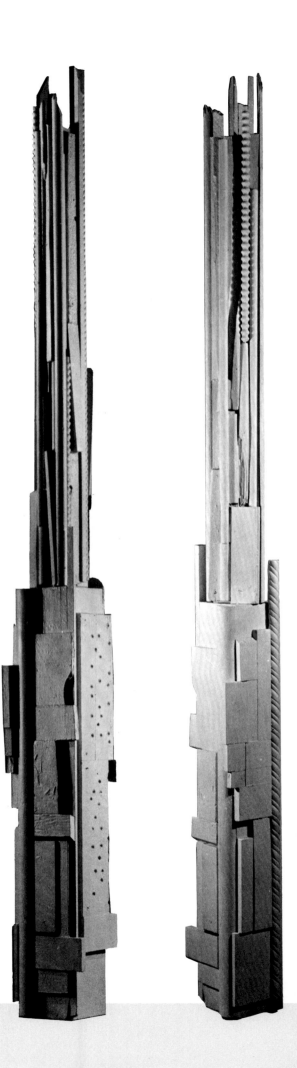

37 *Case with Five Balusters,* 1959
Wood painted white, 28 x 63½ × 8 inches
Martha Jackson Gallery, Inc., New York

38 *Totem II*, 1959
Wood painted white, 110½ x 13½ x 14 inches
Martha Jackson Gallery, Inc., New York

39 *Dawn's Wedding Feast Columns*, 1959
Wood painted white; two columns,
94 x 12 x 9 and 94 x 17 x 9 inches
Menil Foundation, Houston

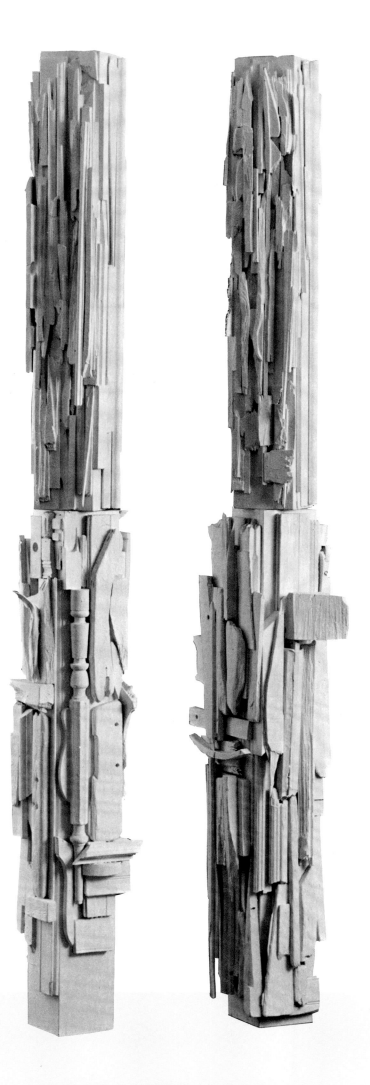

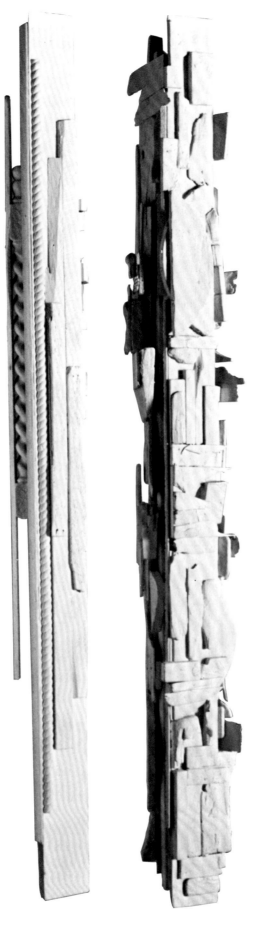

40 *Hanging Columns* (from *Dawn's Wedding Feast*), 1959
Wood painted white; two columns
72 x 6⅝ and 72 x 10⅛ inches
The Museum of Modern Art, New York;
Blanchette Rockefeller Fund

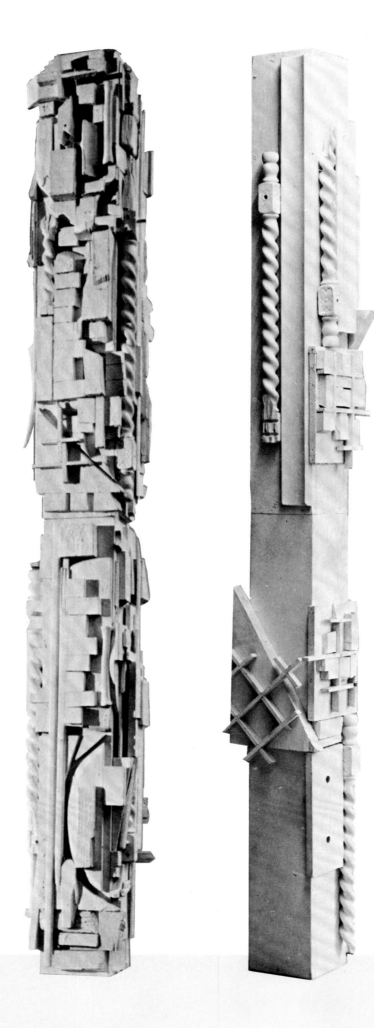

42 *Dawn's Wedding Column*, 1959
Wood painted white, 92½ x 14 x 12⅜ inches
Private collection

43 *Dawn Column I*, 1959
Wood painted white, 92½ x 10½ x 10 inches
William A. Farnsworth Library and
Art Museum, Rockland, Maine

44 *Dawn's Wedding Chapel IV*, 1959–60
Wood painted white, 109 x 87 x 13½ inches
Philippe Braunschweig,
La Chaux-de-Fonds, Switzerland

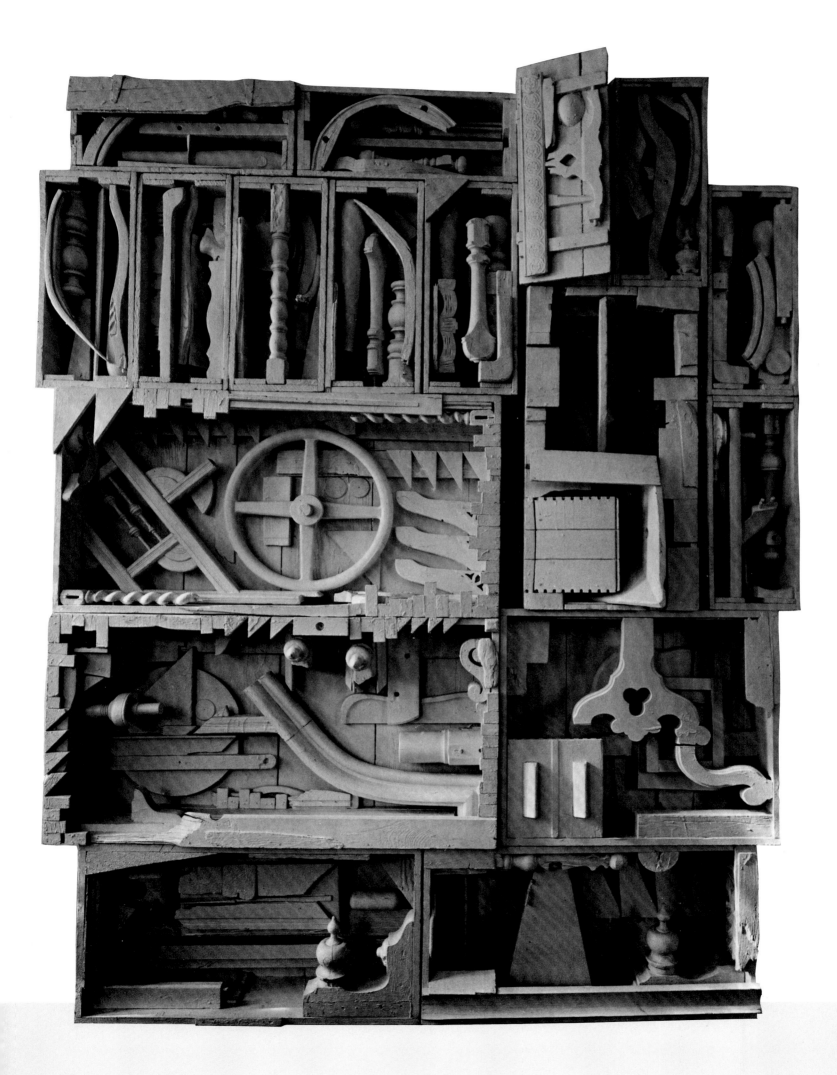

45 *Dawn's Wedding Columns (A and B)*, 1959
Wood painted white; two columns,
59 x 7 x 6 and 60 x 7 x 7¼ inches
The Pace Gallery, New York

46 *America—Dawn*, 1962–67
Wood painted white, 216 x 168 x 120 inches
The Art Institute of Chicago

THE ROYAL TIDES

overleaf
THE ROYAL TIDES
Martha Jackson Gallery, New York
April 20 – May 20, 1961

I walked into the Met one day and they had an exhibition of Japanese Noh robes. Each robe was a universe in itself. Some had gold cloth with medallions and the cloth was so finely woven. It was the reverse of what people think, that gold material is a little vulgar. It was made out of the thinnest of sheer-thin thread, it was so fine. So that the light and shade were of that refinement. Then the medallion was gold . . . so it was gold on gold.

I looked and I sat down without thinking and I had a barrel of tears on the right eye and a barrel of tears on the left eye . . . and then my nose was running . . . and I wanted to go to the bathroom. Everything was open. And then I knew and I said, O my God, life is worth living if a civilization can give us this great weave of gold and pattern. So I sat there and sat and wept and wept and sat.

NOT long after completing "Dawn's Wedding Feast," and again working in separate studios according to the color of the sculpture, Nevelson produced over a dozen walls of gold-painted boxes in less than two years. Some of them were first seen at the Galerie Daniel Cordier in Paris in 1960, and one appeared in the 1960 Whitney Museum Annual Exhibition. Later that year, in an exhibition entitled "The Royal Tides" at the Martha Jackson Gallery, works in gold, as well as black and white, were shown. The focus of the exhibition was the upstairs room that contained two large gold walls, *Royal Tide IV* and *Royal Winds I*; two smaller gold walls, including *Royal Tide I*; a column, and several hanging shields and half moons. Unlike the previous six thematically titled exhibitions, no sculpture stood in the middle of this room. The resplendent gold light from the walls and hovering shields seemed to fill the space, almost overpowering the spectator.

As with the black and the white sculpture, Nevelson transformed society's cast-off and broken shards into elegant compositions of found objects. Sharply angular pieces of scrap wood are played off against some intricately tooled or carved wood objects and furniture parts. In "The Royal Tides," the rounded forms of oval toilet seats and circular picture frames predominated. With an ironic twist, the artist has imposed her own gold standard upon the disparate fragments housed in these shining walls of boxes.

Royal Tide I was included in "The Art of Assemblage," a major exhibition at The Museum of Modern Art in 1961. William Seitz, curator and author of the catalogue, likened this work to an altar, pointing out that beyond the immediacy and tangibility of the forms lay an innate mysticism and romanticism.[6] *Royal Tide I* also marked the beginning of a shift in Nevelson's style, since it was one of the first works in which the artist created a grid out of uniformly sized boxes. Finally in a position to obtain in sufficient quantity both the wood shapes and boxes she sought, she began to have boxes and elements made to order, and to compose works in which numerous, subtly varied repetitions of selected shapes gradually replaced the combinations of randomly collected forms.

Also at this time, Nevelson began to preserve the combination of boxes that made up the walls by screwing them together. Thus, the overall compositions of *Royal Tide IV* and *Royal Tide I* have remained unchanged. *Royal Tide IV* contains a number of identically shaped boxes as well as some furniture parts whose repeated appearances across the wide facade of the wall create a rhythmic pattern which seems deliberate. The artist's finely tuned sense of formal composition has been applied here to the entire wall. This had not been true of the previously exhibited walls of black and of white boxes, and in fact, collectors who owned more than one had been encouraged to move the boxes around at their own discretion.

Among the several themes that have persisted throughout Nevelson's oeuvre, royalty is one of the most prominent. Royal figures were the subject of at least five of the etchings in the 1955 exhibit, "Ancient Games and Ancient Places." The *King* and *Queen of the Sea* were the principal works in "The Royal Voyage" the following year, and even in "Moon Garden + One," a royal figure had been present. *King II*, now part of *Tropical Garden II*, originally stood against the wall to the right of *Sky Cathedral*. Here, in "The Royal Tides," there are no majestic personages, but the aura of magnificence created by these gilded constructions and implied by their titles announces the enduring presence of royalty.

47 Royal Winds I, 1960
Wood painted gold, 132 x 144 x 10 inches
Disassembled

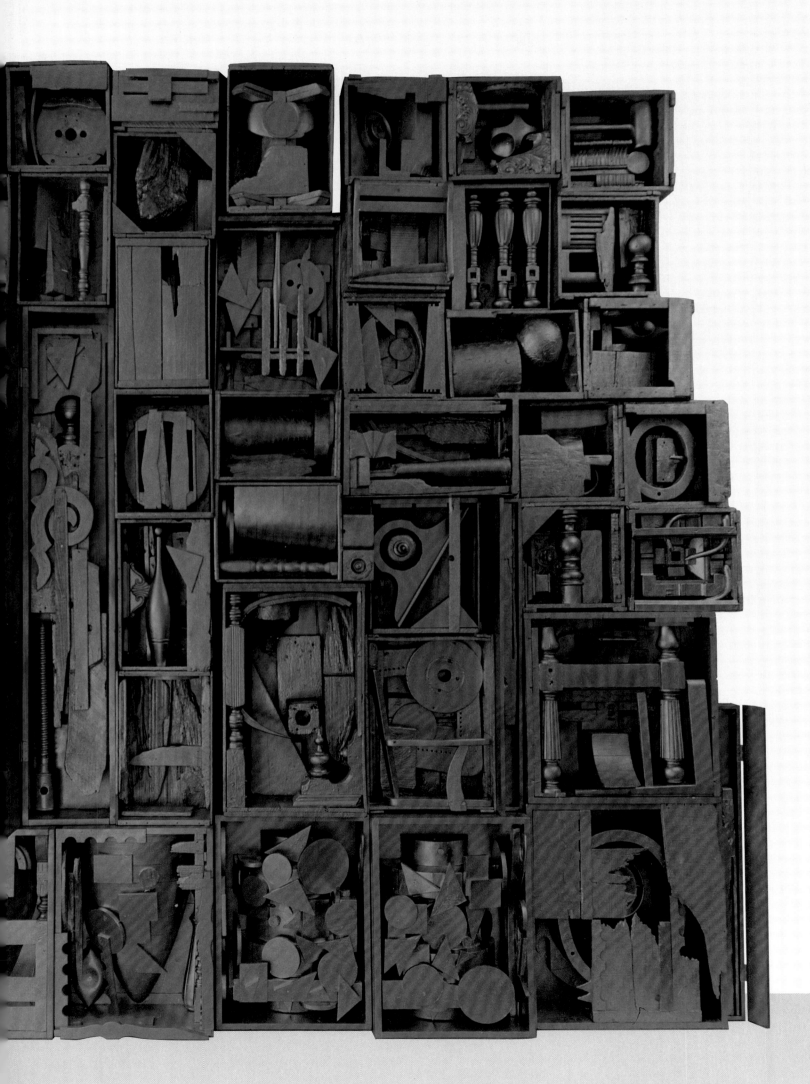

48 *Royal Tide II*, 1961–63
Wood painted gold, 94½ x 126½ x 8 inches
Whitney Museum of American Art, New York;
gift of the artist

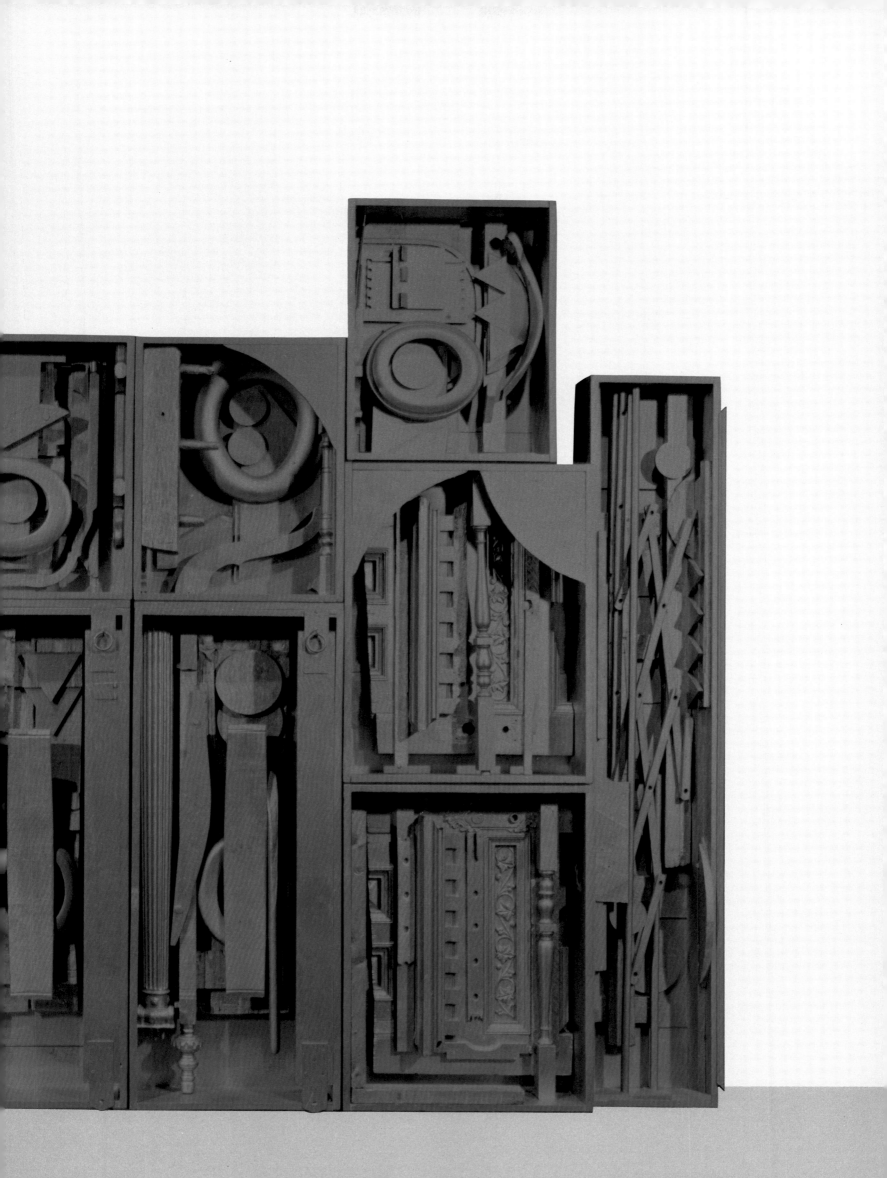

49 *Royal Tide IV*, 1960
Wood painted gold, 132 x 168 x 10 inches
Museum Ludwig, Cologne

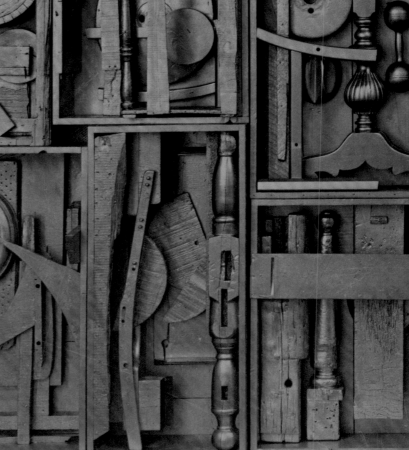

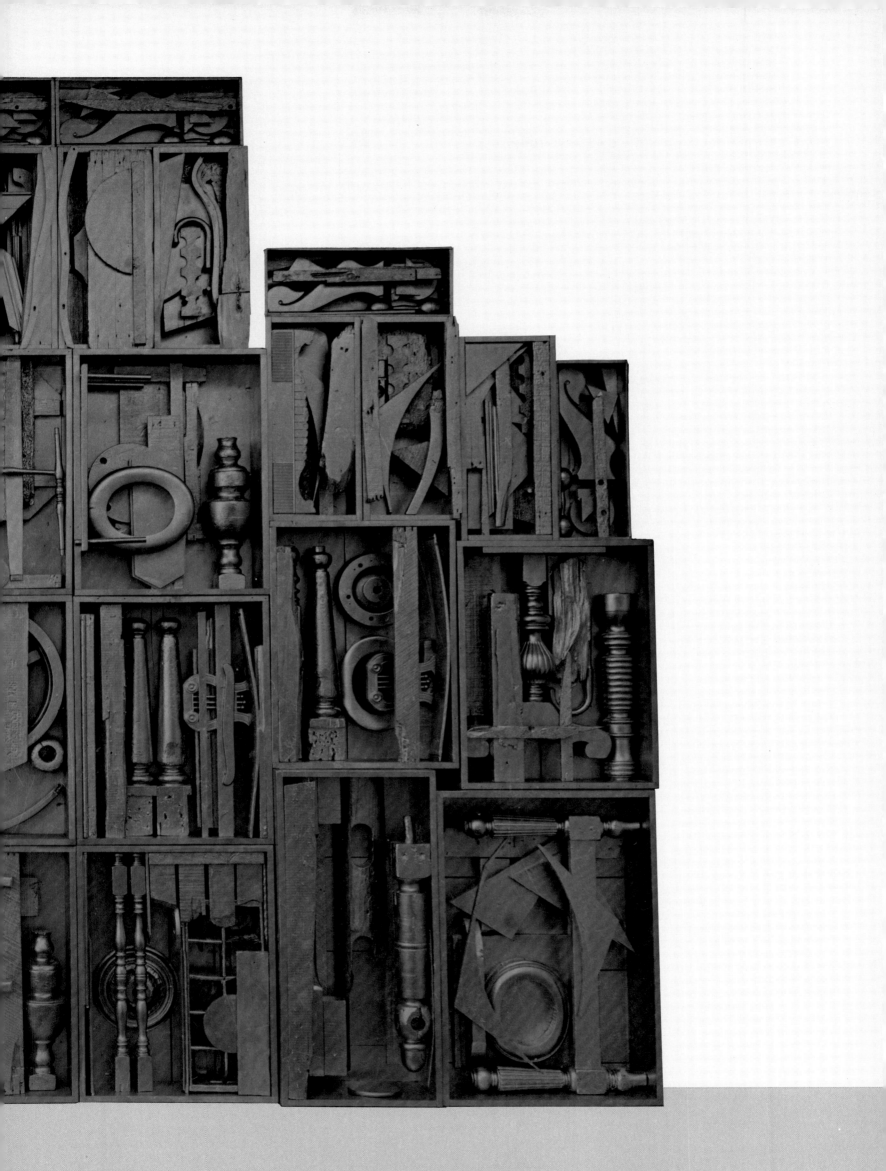

50 *Half Moon II,* 1961
Wood painted gold, 27⅝ x 48⅝ x 2½ inches
Center for the Performing Arts, Smith College,
Northampton, Massachusetts; gift of the Class of 1967

51 *Royal Winds I*, 1960
Wood painted gold,
83 x 46 x 9½ inches
Mr. and Mrs. Kenneth S. Kaiserman,
Philadelphia

52 *Royal Tide III*, 1960
Wood painted gold,
72 x 53 x 10 inches
Private collection

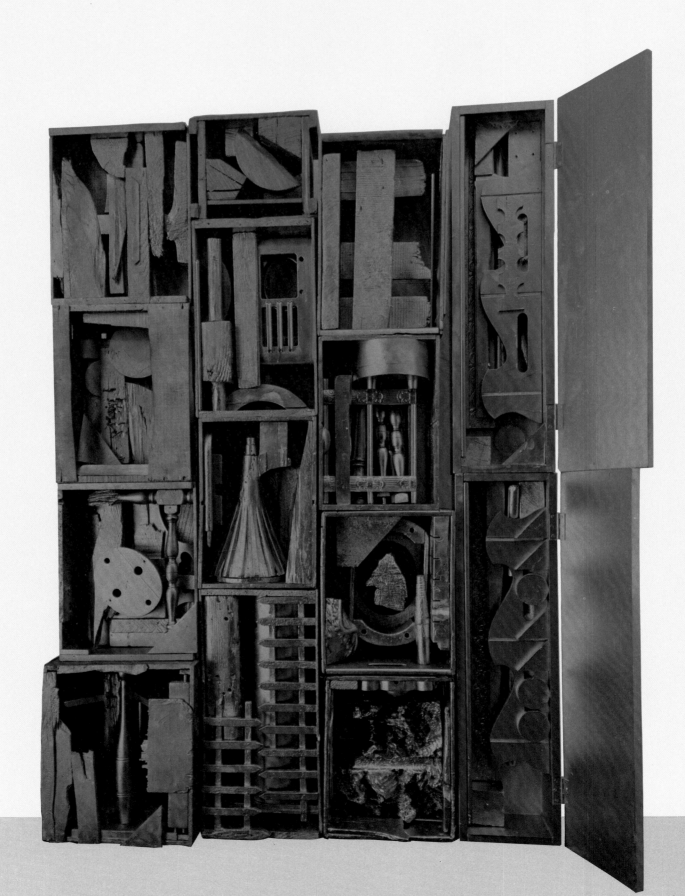

53 *Royal Tide I,* 1960
Wood painted gold,
96 x 40 x 8 inches
Howard and Jean Lipman,
New York

54 *Sun Garden, Number I,* 1964
Wood painted gold; three columns,
72 x 41 x 26 inches overall
Mr. and Mrs. Charles M. Diker,
New York

55 *Royal Tide II*, 1960
Wood painted gold, 54 x 57 x 8 inches
Private collection

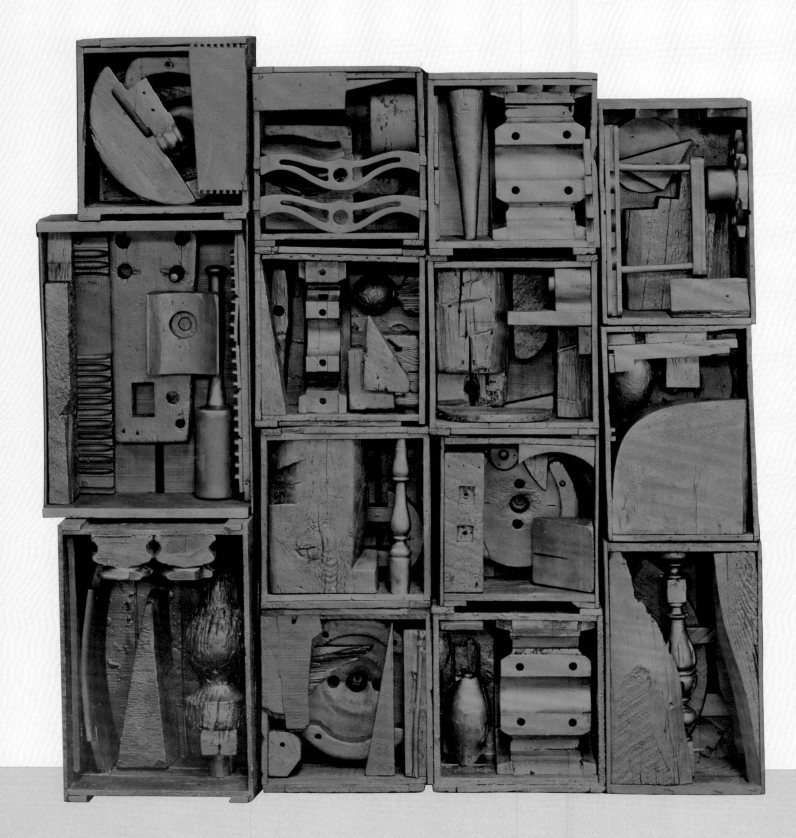

56 Royal Tide Dawn, 1960
Wood painted gold, 91 x 63 x 10⅝ inches
The Pace Gallery, New York

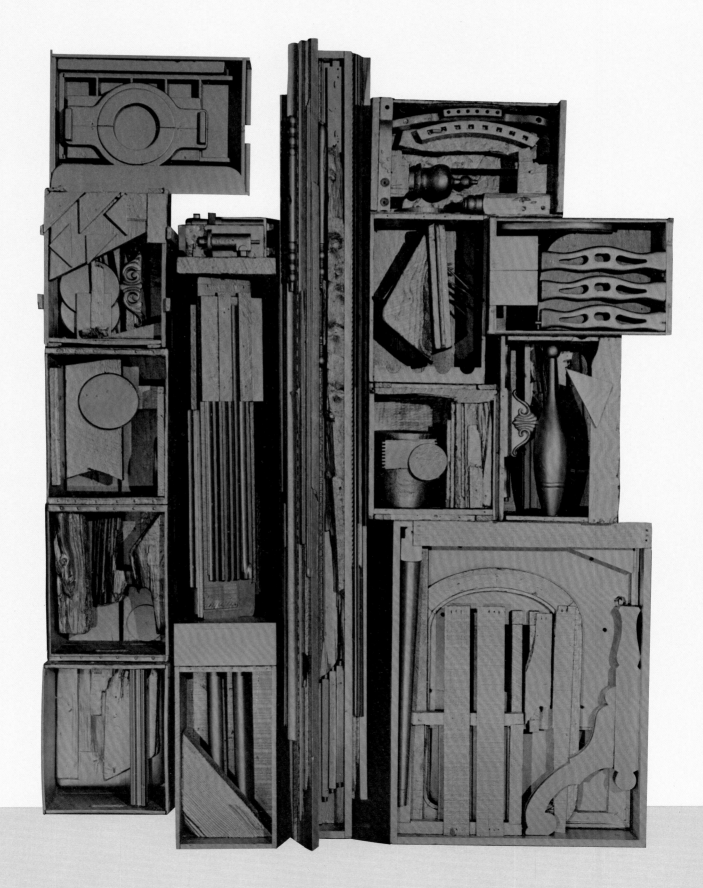

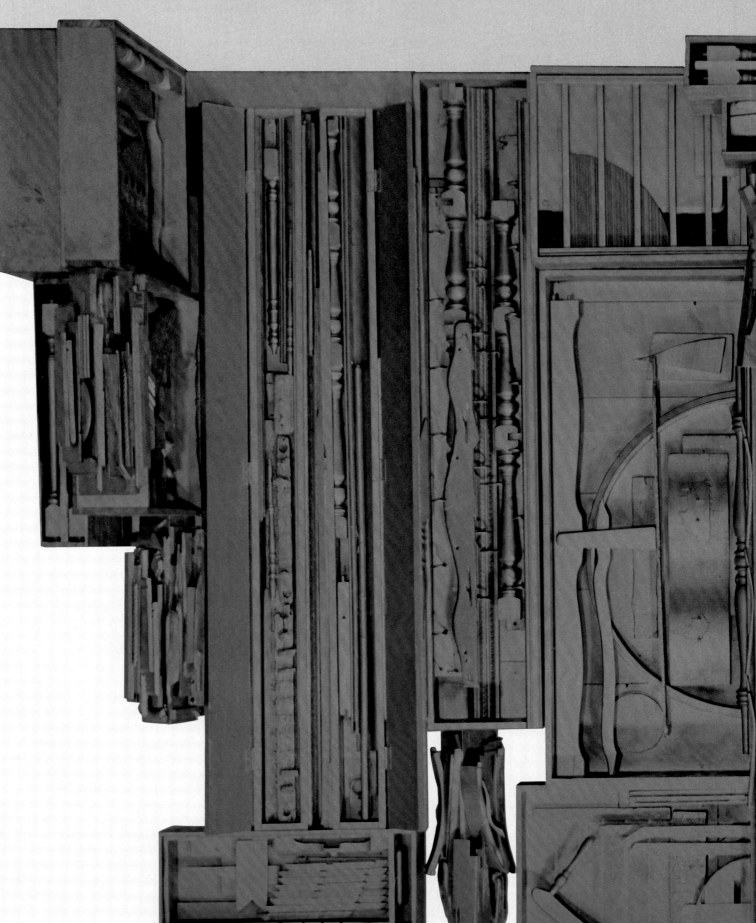

57 *An American Tribute to the British People*, 1960–65
Wood painted gold, 122 x 171 x 42 inches

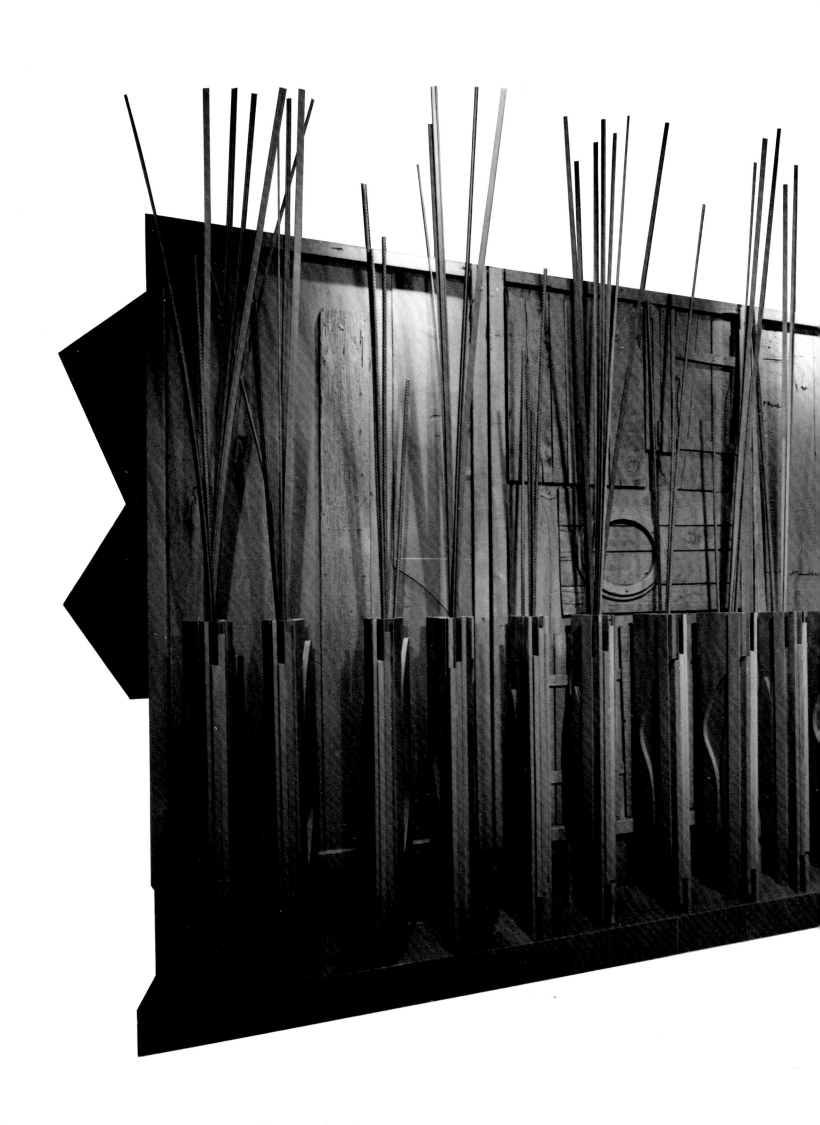

Back view of Mrs. *N's Palace*

I think often people don't realize the meaning of space. They think space is something empty. Actually, in the mind and the projection into this three-dimensional world, space plays the most vital part in our lives. Your concept of what you put into a space will create another space. You can see a person walk into a room and dominate the space. Space has an atmosphere, and what you put into it will color your thinking and your awareness.

Think of placing objects in a space. The size of them, the forms of the pieces, and the color. That is the physical thing. But what about the inner being? The atmosphere? When you sit down and you're in the right place. The effect and reaction. Or when you eat from a certain plate. It can be just a so-called ordinary plate or a very precious plate. But if an object is in the right place, it's enhanced to grandeur. More than that, it pleases the inner being and that, I think, is very important. That equals harmony.

MRS. N'S PALACE (1964–77) is the largest single work Louise Nevelson has ever made, and with it she has realized her long-held wish to create an environment that would remain intact.

Resting on a base of black mirror glass, the wide but shallow structure of the piece is covered, both inside and out, with wood reliefs. Many of these are enclosed in boxes whose varied shapes and sizes enrich the palace walls. On the front and side outer walls the triangles, trapezoids, hexagons, and rectangles of the boxes themselves are joined to form startling rhythms. The boxes vary in depth from a few inches to over a foot deep, and in some places several are superimposed, projecting outward and resting on half-moon-shaped bases. At the rear, long narrow slats and spiral poles grow like tall reeds from two barrels and from a procession of thin vertical containers.

Entering the open doorway, the visitor finds himself in a room which feels surprisingly small. Wood reliefs line the walls, hang from the ceiling, and stand in groups on the reflecting glass floors. They are placed in such a way as to produce narrow interior corridors with incrustations of elegantly composed sculpture. Gradually adjusting to the dimly lit room, the viewer discovers two personages positioned at the right of the entrance. These figures, a king and a queen constructed many years before, had been waiting to find their rightful home.

With the help of Arnold Glimcher, her friend and dealer, and with the aid of two carpenters closely following the artist's instructions, Nevelson built her monumental black-painted wood palace in two weeks. She had long been accumulating the wood elements and they were now installed as part of this magical habitation. Working from a cardboard model, a contractor built the basic structure of the room in a studio space rented especially for it. Her regular studio was then emptied of the accumulated pieces, and she set to work with the great speed, energy, and euphoric mood that have often accompanied her most innovative and powerful work.

As the piece neared completion, she decided upon the title. "Mrs. N" is the name she has been given by the neighborhood children in the Italian section of New York where she has lived for over twenty years. The idea of a palace is far more complex. Again, the theme of royalty is one of the artist's favorites, but the concept of an ideal dwelling place is also a seminal theme in her work. In the late sixties she had hoped to find and convert an East Side brownstone into one large architectural sculpture.[7] Then, inspired by the miniature castle which plays an important and enigmatic role as part of the set in Edward Albee's *Tiny Alice*, Nevelson did a series of small black wood sculptures that she called "dream houses." The first, made in 1972, began with a store-bought doll house which she painted black and decorated with her characteristic compositions of small geometric shapes. Thirty-six other versions of this theme followed and the artist played with various formats, alternating between a horizontal or a vertical orientation, providing many open doors, or a single one with a lock.

With the appearance of *Mrs. N's Palace* five years later, Nevelson enlarged this world and invited the viewer to enter. The gallery announcement for the exhibition read: "Louise Nevelson invites you to Mrs. N's Palace at The Pace Gallery." The king and queen standing inside the doorway greeted the visitors who trod lightly on the black glass floor as they entered the narrow interior space.

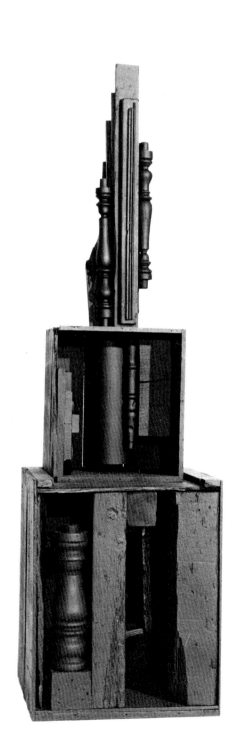

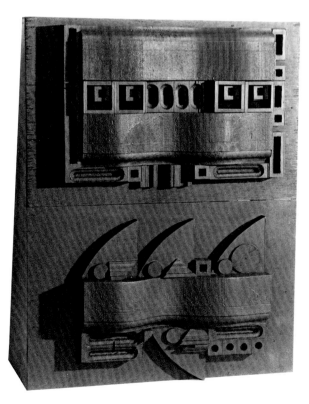

Interior view of *Mrs. N's Palace*

NOTES

1. Louise Nevelson, *Dawns + Dusks,* ed. Diana MacKown (New York: Charles Scribner's Sons, 1976), p. 128.

2. Emily Genauer, *New York Herald Tribune,* 12 January 1958.

3. Press release: "Sky Columns Presence," Louise Nevelson Collection, Archives of American Art, Washington, D.C.

4. Colette Roberts, *Nevelson* (Paris: Editions Georges Fall, 1964), p. 25.

5. Nevelson, *Dawns + Dusks,* p. 138.

6. William Seitz, *The Art of Assemblage* (New York: The Museum of Modern Art, 1961), p. 118.

7. Lisa Hammel, "Louise Nevelson Has Plan for Living: A House That Is One Large Sculpture," *New York Times,* 28 April 1967.

CHRONOLOGY

1899   Louise born in Kiev, Russia, to Isaac
        Berliawsky and Minna Ziesel Smolerank.
        She has an older brother, Nathan, and
        two younger sisters, Anita and Lillian.

1902   Father immigrates to America.

1905   Louise and her family leave Russia to join
        father in America; they settle in
        Rockland, Maine. Her father buys
        woodland, establishes a lumberyard and
        becomes a contractor. Louise attends
        grammar school and high school in
        Rockland.

1918   Graduates from high school. Meets
        Charles Nevelson, a shipowner from New
        York. Becomes engaged soon after.

1920   Marries Charles Nevelson in Boston and
        moves to New York. Travels to New
        Orleans and Cuba on two honeymoon
        trips. During the twenties in New York,
        studies painting and drawing with Theresa
        Bernstein, William Meyerowitz, and the
        Baroness Hilla Rebay; also studies drama
        in Brooklyn at a school founded by
        Princess Matchabelli and Frederick
        Kiesler, and voice with Metropolitan
        Opera coach Estelle Liebling.

1922   Son Myron (Mike) is born.

1928   Begins classes at the Art Students League
        of New York, which she takes for the
        next three years. Studies with Kenneth
        Hayes Miller.

1931   Separates from her husband and travels to
        Munich to study with Hans Hofmann.
        Takes daily drawing classes, but due to
        the political upheavals in Germany,
        Hofmann's participation is infrequent and
        he is forced to close the school six
        months after her arrival. She travels to
        Vienna, where she takes small parts in
        several films. Visits Italy and then Paris,
        where she stays for several weeks,
        spending most of her time in the Louvre
        and the Musée de l'Homme. Begins to
        write poetry. After returning to New
        York, resumes classes at the Art Students
        League.

1932   Meets Diego Rivera through a mutual
        friend and becomes an assistant for his
        series of twenty-one fresco murals, *Portrait
        of America*, done in the New Workers'
        School on Fourteenth Street. Begins to
        study modern dance with Ellen Kearns,
        which she continues into the fifties.
        During the summer, returns to Paris for
        six weeks. After returning to New York,

again takes classes at the Art Students League, studying drawing and painting with Hans Hofmann, now living in New York, and painting with George Grosz.

1934   Exhibits several paintings at the Secession Gallery, New York, her first gallery showing.

1935   One of her terra-cotta figures is included in the exhibition "Young Sculptors" at The Brooklyn Museum, her first museum showing.

1937   Works at painting and sculpture under the Works Progress Administration, and teaches sculpture at the Educational Alliance School of Art in New York.

1941   First one-woman exhibition held at the Nierendorf Gallery, New York, the first gallery to represent her work. Exhibition includes paintings and sculpture made of plaster and clay, mostly done under the WPA. After the show she begins to use found objects in her work.

1943   The first exhibition of sculpture organized around a theme, "The Circus, The Clown Is the Center of His World," is held at the Norlyst Gallery, New York. After the exhibition, she destroys about two hundred paintings and sculpture pieces due to lack of storage space. Buys a house on East Thirtieth Street, New York, made possible by an inheritance from her father, and lives there until 1958. At various times the house becomes a gathering place for artists and organizations such as the Federation of Modern Painters and Sculptors, the Sculptors' Guild, and the Four O'Clock Forum, organized in 1952 by Will Barnet and Steve Wheeler as a forum for aesthetic ideas unrelated to Abstract Expressionism.

1944   First exhibition of abstract wood assemblages is held at the Nierendorf Gallery.

1947   Studies printmaking for the first time with English artist Stanley William Hayter at his workshop, Atelier 17, in New York. Begins a series of etchings, drypoints, and aquatints.

1949   Stops working in wood and produces a series of terra-cotta and marble sculptures, all done at the Sculpture Center on Eighth Street, New York.

1950   During the spring, takes a short trip to Mexico with her sister Anita, visiting the museums in Mexico City. That winter she makes a second trip, visiting the archaeological sites in the Yucatán peninsula, and the Mayan ruins of Quiriguá, Guatemala.

1953   Returns to work at Atelier 17 and finishes the series of prints begun in 1947—thirty prints in all.

1955   "Ancient Games and Ancient Places" shown at Grand Central Moderns, New York, who now represents her work.

1956   "The Royal Voyage (of the King and Queen of the Sea)" shown at Grand Central Moderns.

1957   "The Forest" shown at Grand Central Moderns.
Elected president of the New York chapter of Artists' Equity, a position which she holds for two years.

1958   "Moon Garden + One" shown at Grand Central Moderns.
Sells her house on East Thirtieth Street and moves to a building on Spring Street, where she still lives.

1959   "Sky Columns Presence" shown at Martha Jackson Gallery, New York, who now represents her work.
Creates "Dawn's Wedding Feast," her first white environment, for the exhibition "Sixteen Americans" held at The Museum of Modern Art, New York.

1961   "The Royal Tides" shown at Martha Jackson Gallery.
Elected president of National Artists' Equity.

1962   Selected as one of three artists to represent the United States at the XXXI Biennale Internazionale d'Arte, Venice. Creates a black, a white, and a gold environment for three rooms in the United States Pavilion.

Wins Grand Prize of $3,000 in the First Sculpture International at the Torcuato di Tella Institute's Center of Visual Arts, Buenos Aires.

1963   Receives a Ford Foundation grant to work at the Tamarind Lithography Workshop in Los Angeles. Produces twenty-six prints.

1964   Begins affiliation with The Pace Gallery, New York.

1966   First metal sculptures are fabricated from aluminum.

1967   Retrospective exhibition held at the Whitney Museum of American Art, New York.
Small Plexiglas sculptures are begun and made in multiples through the next year.
Returns to the Tamarind Lithography Workshop and produces a series of sixteen prints.

1969   *Atmosphere and Environment X,* the first large-scale cor-ten steel sculpture, is commissioned by Princeton University.
Retrospective exhibition held at The Museum of Fine Arts, Houston.

1970   Begins a series of lead intaglio relief prints and continues through the next three years; six prints are produced in all.

1971   Produces a series of sculptures, *Seventh Decade Garden,* made from direct-welded aluminum scraps.
Receives a Creative Arts Award in Sculpture from Brandeis University.
Awarded the Skowhegan Medal for Sculpture.

1972   Continues large outdoor cor-ten steel sculptures: *Night Presence IV* is installed on Park Avenue at Ninety-second Street, New York; *Atmosphere and Environment XIII (Windows to the West)* is installed in Scottsdale, Arizona.

1973   Walker Art Center, Minneapolis, organizes a retrospective exhibition of wood sculpture; exhibition travels to five museums in the United States.

1975   *Bicentennial Dawn,* the largest wood sculpture to date, commissioned for the

James A. Byrne Federal Courthouse, Philadelphia.
Transparent Horizon, a cor-ten steel sculpture, is commissioned for the Massachusetts Institute of Technology by I. M. Pei.

1976   Exhibits pieces from "Moon Garden + One" at the Biennale di Venezia.
Included in the exhibition "200 Years of American Sculpture" at the Whitney Museum of American Art.
Sky Tree, cor-ten steel, installed in the Embarcadero Center in San Francisco.

1977   Creates a series of white sculptures for the interior of the Chapel of the Good Shepherd in Saint Peter's Church, New York.
Mrs. N's Palace shown at The Pace Gallery.

1978   Legion Memorial Square, in the Wall Street area of Manhattan, is renamed Louise Nevelson Plaza. Seven large metal sculptures, *Shadows and Flags,* are installed there.
Sky Gate — New York, cor-ten steel, is made for the World Trade Center, New York.

1979   A group of three large cor-ten steel sculptures, *The Bendix Trilogy,* is installed in Southfield, Michigan.
Receives the President's Medal of the Municipal Art Society of New York.
Elected to membership in the American Academy of Arts and Letters. Occupies Chair Two, originally held by Augustus Saint-Gaudens.

BIBLIOGRAPHY

ANCIENT GAMES AND ANCIENT PLACES
Grand Central Moderns, New York
January 8–25, 1955

B[urrey], S[uzanne]. "Fortnight in Review: Nevelson," *Arts Digest*, 29 (1 January 1955), p. 21.

O'H[ara], F[rank]. "Reviews and Previews: Sculpture 1955." *Art News*, 54 (September 1955), p. 51.

P[orter], F[airfield]. "Reviews and Previews: Louise Nevelson." *Art News*, 53 (January 1955), p. 46.

"Ancient Games and Ancient Places best of all illustrates that art is for her a possibility that she sees in everything, as a child playing does not distinguish his crayons and toys from the grown-up furniture."

Preston, Stuart. "Recent Sculpture and Painting: Abstract and Figurative." *New York Times*, 16 January 1955, section 2, p. 11.

THE ROYAL VOYAGE (OF THE KING AND QUEEN OF THE SEA)
Grand Central Moderns, New York
February 18–March 8, 1956

M[ellow], J[ames] R. "In the Galleries: Personages at Sea." *Arts*, 30 (February 1956), p. 52.
"As part of her exhibition, the theme of which is 'The King and Queen of the Sea,' Mrs. Nevelson exhibits this collection of attendant black upright shapes — each given lateral equality on common level ground; the beauty of each defined by relationship with its neighboring forms; the character of each made more explicit by nicks, splits, gouges and other minor scars and accidents of time. This one piece, assembled with others, forms a small universe of sentinel shapes charged with personality."

Munro, Eleanor. "Explorations in Form." *Perspectives USA*, Summer 1956, pp. 160–72.

T[yler], P[arker]. "Reviews and Previews: Louise Nevelson." *Art News*, 54 (February 1956), pp. 48–49.
"Her present show, like her last, is based on a theme. Now it is also poetic: 'The King and Queen of the Sea.' Much more like posts than people, the King is more of a solid piece; the Queen, perforated. Their domain closely resembles them though at a disadvantage in scale. It is a suite of variations on height and thickness, number and relation, created with a certain spare but gracious inevitability. Black, immediate as a profile, each work — like a fragile melody — must be experienced more than once to learn all its virtues: an oblique look brings out an incidental shaved plane, a human face etched on the wood, natural splits like human wrinkles. The feminine delicacy she achieves is that her melodic images have an illusory distance, a grouping

mysteriously intangible, and a limited dynamic balance illustrated by the tiny spaces frequently separating their internal units. The sculptural *corps* is played on in these works as the mind plays with memory."

THE FOREST

Grand Central Moderns, New York
January 4–23, 1957

A[shton], D[ore]. "Art: Forest Sculptures; Pieces Hewn in Wood by Louise Nevelson Evoke Arboreal Metaphors." *New York Times*, 8 January 1957, p. 34.

"This ensemble of sculptures hewn in wood evokes, in its unity, a host of metaphors for forest life. . . . There are many presences. A giant piece, 'The Tender Being,' a sharp profile with gentle modeling within . . . assumes the magic of a presence. . . . First personage, an enormous looming shape which does seem to be . . . a primordial image. Many of Miss Nevelson's works are assembled from separately carved members in a system of rhythmic horizontals and verticals. . . . In her inventive use of wood covering, her sublimation of detail to the whole, Miss Nevelson is a forceful sculptor."

Kramer, Hilton. "Month in Review." *Arts*, 31 (January 1957), pp. 44–47.

"In the new wood constructions, all stained to a uniform black which varies only texturally and as the light falls upon its great multiplicity of surfaces, it is indeed a world of darkness which is evoked. A characteristic work reveals an accumulation of these dark bulky forms gathered together on a pedestal; each of these, whether rough or smooth, complex in outline or starkly simplified, whether massive or linear, will be found to hold an expressive as well as an architectural relation to its co-occupants on the pedestal. And while the creative process here is an additive one, the finished whole—both in imagery and effect—is artistically larger than the sum of the parts. . . . One must really enter the shadows here before one can *see*."

P[orter], F[airfield]. "Reviews and Previews: Louise Nevelson." *Art News*, 55 (January 1957), pp. 23–24.

MOON GARDEN + ONE

Grand Central Moderns, New York
January 4–23, 1958

B[aldwin], C[arl]. "In the Galleries: Louise Nevel-

son." *Arts*, 32 (January 1958), p. 55.

"Perhaps 'enclosures' is more adequate a word than 'sculptures' to describe these works on the theme of *Moon Garden*. The artist . . . explores a kind of twilight kingdom where night suns and day moons reveal treasured objects sheltered in chests or tall boxes."

Genauer, Emily. "Abstract Art with Meaning: A World." *New York Herald Tribune*, 12 January 1958, section 6, p. 14.

Kramer, Hilton. "The Sculpture of Louise Nevelson." *Arts*, 32 (June 1958), pp. 26–29.

"What does seem to occupy her most . . . is the impulse to project on a macrocosmic scale the artistic vision which is embodied in each given work. Often in these exhibitions the integrity of the individual work is totally sacrificed to the interest in constructing this macrocosmic vision in the gallery itself. Each exhibition is assigned a title as if it were a singular conception. The individual sculpture becomes a unit in the larger design; and the entire ensemble is made to assume an expressive power perhaps greater than—but always directly related to—the essential sculptural idea which animates each work. . . . In her most recent exhibition . . . nearly every conceivable demand was made on the gallery space. It was entirely transformed into a continuous sculptural enclosure, dominated by an enormous wall-sculpture, which in itself represented a brilliant realization of everything toward which Mrs. Nevelson has been aspiring in her recent efforts: neither a relief nor a construction to hang on the wall, but an *actual wall*, in the literal, architectural sense, which was at the same time a work of sculpture."

"Art: One Woman's World." *Time*, 3 February 1958, p. 58.

"Sculptress Louise Nevelson . . . waves a nervous hand at the shapes and explains: 'This is the universe, the stars, the moon—and you and I, everyone. . . . This is *Cathedral in the Sky*, man's temple to man. And over there is the *Moon Dial*, the clocking of man's eternal search for the serene. Behind it, the *Heavenly Gate*, and above it, the *Cross*. But I'm not talking about Christianity. I speak of total being. . . . I plan my shows as an ensemble, as one work. Everything has to fit together, to flow without effort, and I too must fit.'"

[Seiberling, Dorothy]. "Weird Woodwork of Lunar World." *Life*, 24 March 1958, pp. 77–80.

"The Moon Garden is composed of 116 boxes and

circular shapes stacked or standing free. They are filled or covered with odds and ends of wood. The 57-year-old artist, who is the daughter of a Maine lumberman, scavenged the wood from beaches, demolished houses, and antique shops and has cut or shaped it to her own desire. Everything is painted black because, says Miss Nevelson, 'black creates harmony and doesn't intrude on the emotions.' The entire Moon Garden was priced at $18,000. But since most gallerygoers didn't relish living totally in the dark of the moon, Miss Nevelson parted with individual boxes for as little as $95. Seven were sold."

T[yler], P[arker]. "Reviews and Previews: Louise Nevelson." *Art News*, 56 (January 1958), p. 54.
"Subtle shifts in relief, lidded box composition and free-standing figures make a constant esthetic event in itself because the show's elements comprise a single 'landscape' dominated by a 'cathedral' of tiered units. Divided between stark austerity and a 'Gothic' lyricism, these works proclaim the dexterity of a rare formal passion."

SKY COLUMNS PRESENCE

Martha Jackson Gallery, New York
October 28 – November 21, 1959

"Art: Adventurous Sculptress." *Newsweek*, 9 November 1959, p. 119.

Ashton, Dore. "Art: Worlds of Fantasy; Louise Nevelson's Sculpture at Jackson Gallery — Works by Richenberg Shown." *New York Times*, 29 October 1959, p. 54.

S[awin], M[artica]. "In the Galleries: Louise Nevelson." *Arts*, 34 (December 1959), p. 57.
"A wall running the length of the gallery was covered by Nevelson boxes, piled floor to ceiling and overflowing around the corner, while clusters of free-standing and suspended columns and isolated units filled the floor space and hung on the opposite wall. The light was so subdued that one really had to peer to see more than the shadowed silhouette of any piece, except on the wall of stacked boxes, where red and green spotlights turned the black to an eerie silvery gray. . . . What the artist wants us to see is the room, the sum of the parts, not the fragment, although she has lavished attention on each part. So — how does it feel, wandering for an interval in this Nevelson world? It is hushed and almost compels one to whisper, as if there were concealed listeners behind the open and shut doors of the columns or in the dark recesses of the boxes."

S[chuyler], J[ames]. "Reviews and Previews: Louise Nevelson." *Art News*, 58 (December 1959), p. 19.
"The mat black that robs elements of local color (and its implicit nostalgia) converts them into a new medium, a kind of porous bronze. The overt and three-dimensional theatricality carried all the way becomes, not an imposed artifice, but a convention gladly accepted for the proliferating fresh surprises."

DAWN'S WEDDING FEAST

The Museum of Modern Art, New York
December 16, 1959 – February 14, 1960

Adlow, Dorothy. "'Sixteen Americans,' a Vigorous Display." *Christian Science Monitor*, 19 December 1959, p. 10.

Canaday, John. Review in *New York Times*, 31 January 1960, section 2.

Coates, Robert M. "The Art Galleries." *New Yorker*, 2 January 1960, p. 61.
"Her contribution here consists of a set of twelve pieces — a sort of abstract reredos or altar, large and complex; a wall construction suggesting an oriel window; a bridal pair; a group of spectators (I am offering my own interpretations) — under the common title of 'Dawn's Wedding Feast.' Spaced about as they are, and colored a uniform white, they give the room they are in an overwhelming feeling of cathedral silence and calm."

Genauer, Emily. "Art: Some Rediscoveries; Experiments of the Present Form Our View of the Past." *New York Herald Tribune*, 20 December 1959, section 4, p. 8.

Hess, Thomas B. "U.S. Art, Notes from 1960." *Art News*, 58 (January 1960), pp. 25–29, 56–58.
"Hers is a splendid room of snow newels, finials, slats, knobs, dowels, mitered corners, lintels, studs and maybe an old croquet set. The snow is milky paint. There is a sense that a whole environment has succumbed to an artist's iron will and velvet eyes."

Kuh, Katherine. "The Fine Arts: A Contemporary Canvass of the American Canvas." *Saturday Review*, 23 January 1960, pp. 29, 40.

Schwartz, M. D. "Sixteen Americans at The Museum of Modern Art." *Apollo*, 71 (February 1960), pp. 49–50.
"It came as something of a surprise to see the group at the museum entirely in white, but the explanation

probably lies in its title, *Dawn's Wedding Feast*. It is monumental, consisting of relief and free-standing constructions filled with delightful patterned elements, old banister balusters, bits of moulding, and finials used with rougher elements. The sensitivity revealed in the choice of pieces to be used together is striking."

THE ROYAL TIDES

Martha Jackson Gallery, New York
April 20 – May 20, 1961

"Art: All That Glitters." *Time,* 31 August 1962, p. 40.

"In another room, shallow honeycombs of orange-crate cabinetry are filled with carefully posed objects—chair legs, a broken wheel, a bowling pin, parts of a table pedestal, a banister, some toilet seats—all gleaming goldly. . . . Besides the three rooms of golden debris in her house, she maintains two more studios near by—one in a former pizzeria, where she does her 'dirty work, my black things,' and one a few doors away for her white work. . . . She denies that she is presently in a gold period, although most of her work, after being lacquered with several coats to seal the wood, is lavishly spray-bombed with a metallic product called Spray-O-Namel."

Ashton, Dore. "Art." *Arts & Architecture,* 78 (June 1961), pp. 4–5.

K[roll], J[ack]. "Reviews and Previews: Louise Nevelson." *Art News,* 60 (May 1961), pp. 10–11.

Raynor, Vivian. "In the Galleries: Louise Nevelson." *Arts Magazine,* 35 (September 1961), p. 40.

"Whether it is because her latest constructions are sprayed with gold paint, or whether the ingredients are becoming more ornate, she seems to be entering a baroque phase, and seems also to be working on a larger scale. The pigeonholes of the 'walls' are perhaps fuller, and one thought there were more claw-and-balls among their contents, all of which seem to have started out in the statelier homes. But they could never have looked as august and glistening as they do now, transfixed by the Nevelson spell."

MRS. N'S PALACE

The Pace Gallery, New York
November 26, 1977 – January 7, 1978

Cavaliere, Barbara. "Louise Nevelson." *Arts Magazine,* 52 (February 1978), p. 32.

Foster, Hal. "Reviews: New York." *Artforum,* February 1978, p. 68.

Hughes, Robert. "Art: Night and Silence, Who Is There?" *Time,* 12 December 1977, pp. 59–60.

"It is addressed, above all, to mystery. Unified by the black paint, the thousands of objects that make up *Mrs. N's Palace* shed their identity. They do not become sinister—this is no mere haunted house—but they do become less knowable, withdrawn from recognition within the austere space of Nevelson's fiction. . . . Collection, repetition, unification: these are the elements of Nevelson's poetic but wholly sculptural sensibility, and this time they have produced a masterpiece."

Kramer, Hilton. "Art: A Nevelson Made to Last." *New York Times,* 9 December 1977, p. C17.

"Physically constructed of wood that is painted black, it is visually an intricate structure of shadow and light. Its complex interior, lighted from within, rests on a black mirror surface that serves as both a floor and a base, while its four external sides—a facade divided by an entrance, two side walls and a back 'garden'—provide a continually absorbing anthology of Mrs. Nevelson's characteristic forms. In many respects a summation of everything the artist has attempted in the last quarter-century, 'Mrs. N's Palace' is also important in another respect. Beginning with her exhibitions in the 1950's, Mrs. Nevelson always showed her work in a special way—as an enclosed and continuous environment constructed of sculptural objects. These environments generated an atmosphere of mystery and romance—a very personal and dramatic sculptural dream world not soon forgotten by anyone who saw them. . . . If one had to choose one work that contains the essence of her achievement, this would be it, and is clearly intended to be it. It is an experience not to be missed."

Schwartz, Ellen. "Two from Nevelson: A Stunning Chapel and a Palace for the Child in All of Us." *Art News,* 77 (February 1978), pp. 54–55.

Zimmer, William. "Nevelson's Palace." *SoHo Weekly News,* 15 December 1977, p. 26.

SELECTED BOOKS, CATALOGUES, AND PERIODICALS

Ashton, Dore. "U.S.A.: Louise Nevelson." *Cimaise,* April–June 1960, pp. 26–36.

Baro, Gene. *Nevelson: The Prints.* New York: Pace Editions, 1974.

Baur, John I. H. *Nature in Abstraction*. New York: Whitney Museum of American Art and the Macmillan Company, 1958.

Friedman, Martin. *Nevelson Wood Sculptures*. New York: E. P. Dutton, 1973.

Glimcher, Arnold B. *Louise Nevelson*. New York: Praeger Publishers, Inc., 1972.

Gordon, John. *Louise Nevelson*. New York: Whitney Museum of American Art and Praeger Publishers, Inc., 1967.

Johnson, Una E. *Louise Nevelson*. New York: Shorewood Publishers, Inc., 1967.

Kramer, Hilton. "Art." *The Nation*, 26 January 1963, pp. 78–79.

Louise Nevelson. Paris: Galerie Daniel Gervis, 1967.

Louise Nevelson. Rockland, Maine: William A. Farnsworth Library and Art Museum, 1979.

Louise Nevelson: First London Exhibition. London: Hanover Gallery, 1963.

Miller, Dorothy C., ed. *Sixteen Americans*. New York: The Museum of Modern Art, 1959.

Nevelson. New York: Martha Jackson Gallery, 1961.

Nevelson: Recent Wood Sculpture. New York: The Pace Gallery, 1969.

Nevelson: Recent Wood Sculpture. New York: The Pace Gallery, 1977.

Nevelson: Sky Gates and Collages. New York: The Pace Gallery, 1974.

Nevelson, Louise. "Queen of the Black Black." In Philip Pearlstein, "The Private Myth." *Art News*, September 1961, p. 45.

————. "A Fairy Tale," in Colette Roberts, *Nevelson*. Paris: Editions Georges Fall, 1964.

————. Statement in "Period Rooms — The Sixties and Seventies." *Art in America*, November – December 1970, p. 129.

————. "Do Your Work," in "Why Have There Been No Great Women Artists?" *Art News*, January 1971, pp. 41–43.

————. "Nevelson on Nevelson." *Art News*, November 1972, pp. 66–68.

————. *Dawns + Dusks*. Edited by Diana Mac-Kown. New York: Charles Scribner's Sons, 1976.

Roberts, Colette. *Nevelson*. Paris: Editions Georges Fall, 1964.

Rosenblum, Robert. "Louise Nevelson." *Arts Yearbook 3: Paris/New York*, 1959, pp. 136–39.

Seckler, Dorothy Gees. "Louise Nevelson." *Art in America*, January – February 1967, pp. 32–43.

Seitz, William. *The Art of Assemblage*. New York: The Museum of Modern Art, 1961.

————. *2 Pittori 2 Scultori*. Organized for the XXXI Venice Biennale by the International Council of The Museum of Modern Art, New York, 1962.

DIAGRAMS OF THE ENVIRONMENTS

DRAWINGS BY PATRICIA WYNNE

Diagrams of the environments are as accurate as possible, based on existing photographs of the original installations. When known, titles of works are given. Plate references are given for those works, or for related works, illustrated elsewhere in this book.

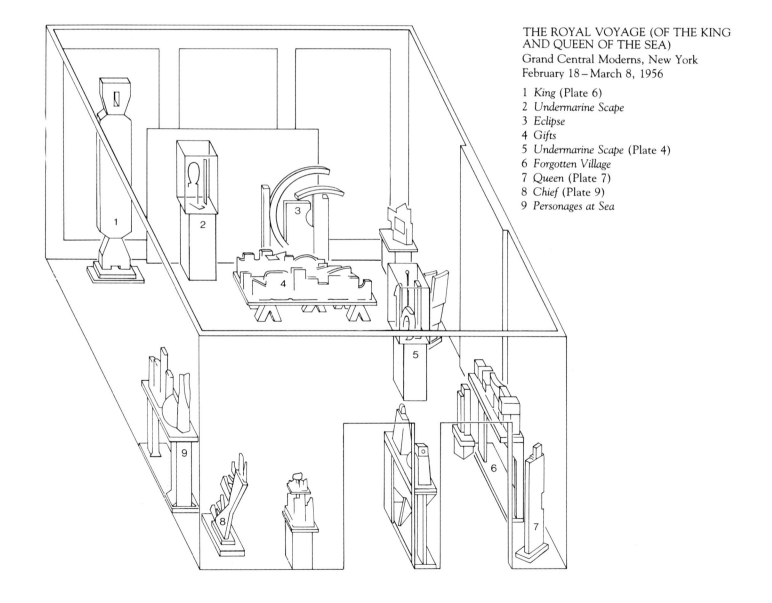

THE ROYAL VOYAGE (OF THE KING AND QUEEN OF THE SEA)
Grand Central Moderns, New York
February 18 – March 8, 1956

1 *King* (Plate 6)
2 *Undermarine Scape*
3 *Eclipse*
4 *Gifts*
5 *Undermarine Scape* (Plate 4)
6 *Forgotten Village*
7 *Queen* (Plate 7)
8 *Chief* (Plate 9)
9 *Personages at Sea*

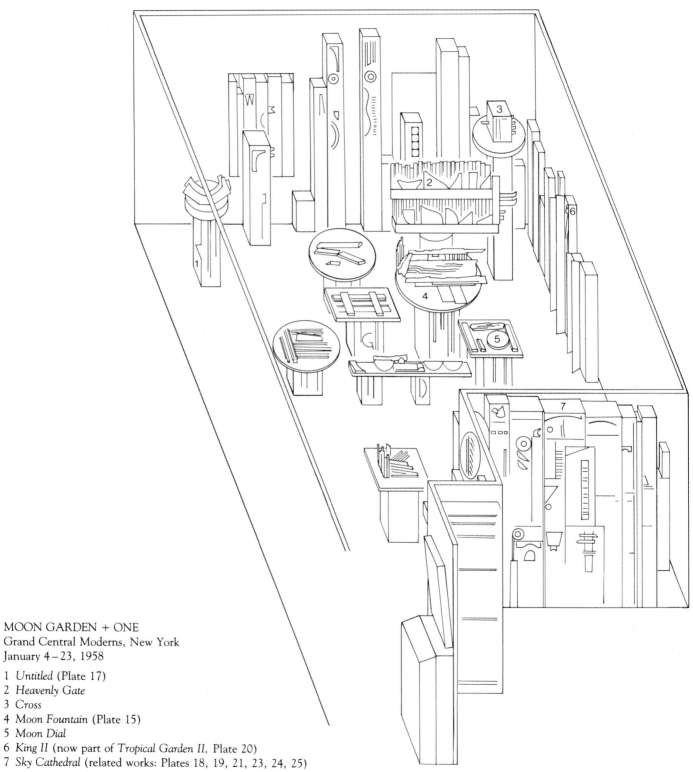

MOON GARDEN + ONE
Grand Central Moderns, New York
January 4 – 23, 1958

1 *Untitled* (Plate 17)
2 *Heavenly Gate*
3 *Cross*
4 *Moon Fountain* (Plate 15)
5 *Moon Dial*
6 *King II* (now part of *Tropical Garden II*, Plate 20)
7 *Sky Cathedral* (related works: Plates 18, 19, 21, 23, 24, 25)

DAWN'S WEDDING FEAST
The Museum of Modern Art, New York
December 16, 1959 – February 14, 1960

1 *Case with Five Balusters* (Plate 37)
2 *Dawn's Wedding Mirror* (Plate 30)
3 *Dawn's Wedding Chest* (Plate 32)
4 *Dawn's Wedding Chapel* (related works: Plates 28, 29, 44)
5 *Dawn's Wedding Columns* (related works: Plates 34, 35, 38, 39, 42, 43)
6 *Dawn's Wedding Pillow* (Plate 33)
7 *Sun Disc* (Plate 41)
8 *Dawn Lake* (Plate 36)
9 *Dawn's Wedding Columns* (related works: Plates 40, 45)
10 *Untitled* (now part of *America—Dawn*, Plate 46)

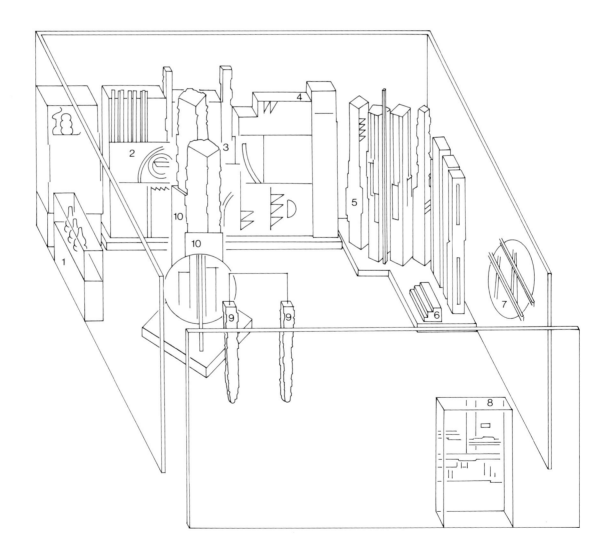

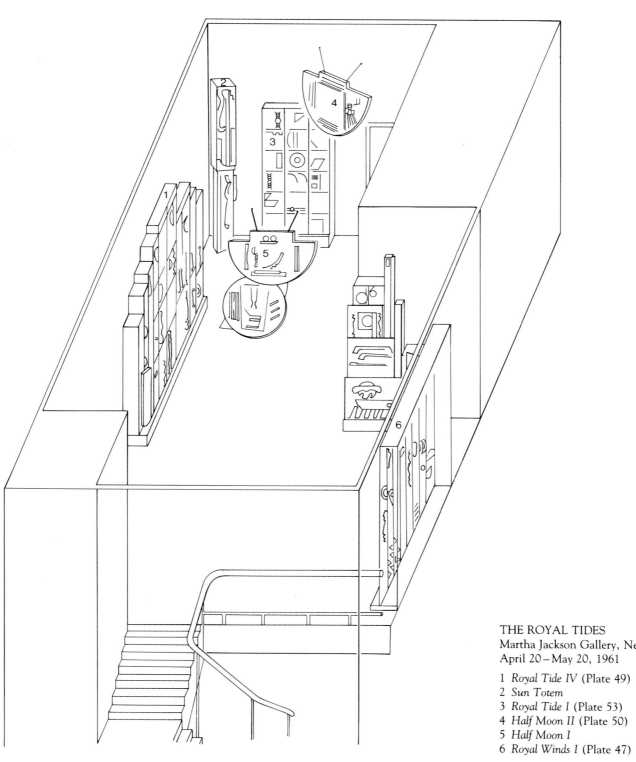

THE ROYAL TIDES
Martha Jackson Gallery, New York
April 20 – May 20, 1961

1 *Royal Tide IV* (Plate 49)
2 *Sun Totem*
3 *Royal Tide I* (Plate 53)
4 *Half Moon II* (Plate 50)
5 *Half Moon I*
6 *Royal Winds I* (Plate 47)

MRS. N'S PALACE
The Pace Gallery, New York
November 26, 1977 – January 7, 1978

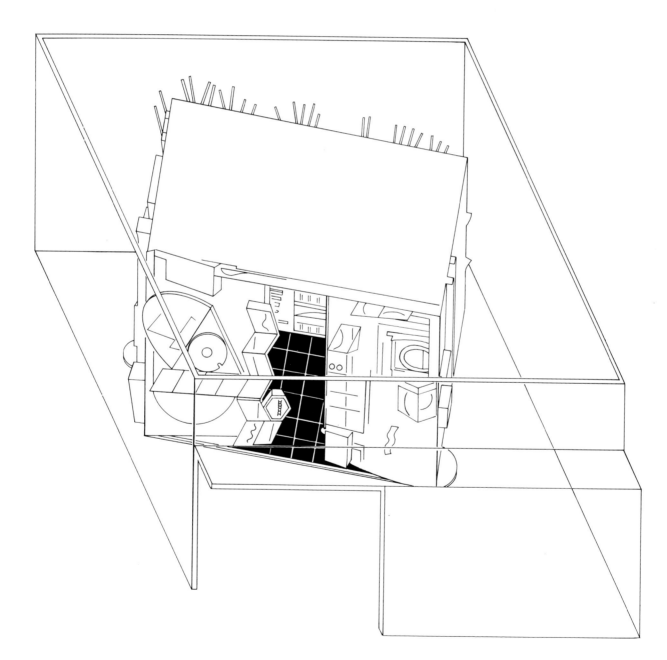

WORKS IN THE EXHIBITION

Photographs unavailable for six of the works.

THE ROYAL VOYAGE

Moon Spikes, ca. 1953
Wood painted black, 17 x 54 x 9″
The Pace Gallery, New York
Plate 1

Moon Spikes, ca. 1953
Wood painted black, 18 x 43 x 5″
The Pace Gallery, New York

Black Horizontal, 1954
Wood painted black, 10 x 68½ x 6½″
Private collection

Black Majesty, 1955
Wood painted black, 28 x 32 x 19″
Whitney Museum of American Art,
New York; gift of Mr. and Mrs. Ben Mildwoff
through the Federation of Modern Painters
and Sculptors, Inc.
Plate 2

Chief, 1955
Wood painted black, 48 x 27 x 8¼″
Barrett N. Linde, Washington, D.C.
Plate 9

Forgotten City, 1955
Wood painted black, 85¾ x 30¾ x 11¼"
Grey Art Gallery and Study Center,
New York University Art Collection;
gift of Mrs. Anita Berliawsky
Plate 8

Night Presence VI, 1955
Wood painted black, 11 x 33 x 8½"
Mrs. Vivian Merrin, New York
Plate 12

Standing Figure, ca. 1955–57
Wood painted black, 69⅝ x 14⅛ x 12"
Hirshhorn Museum and Sculpture Garden,
Smithsonian Institution, Washington, D.C.

East River City Scape, 1956
Wood painted black, 23 x 30½ x 16"
Weatherspoon Art Gallery,
University of North Carolina at Greensboro
Plate 11

First Personage, 1956
Wood painted black; two sections,
94 x 37 x 11¼" and 74 x 24¼ x 7¼"
The Brooklyn Museum, New York;
gift of Mr. and Mrs. Nathan Berliawsky
Plate 13

King, 1956 (reconstructed 1979)
Wood painted black, 117 x 10 x 8"
Collection of the artist

Night Music, 1956
Wood painted black, 13½ x 13 x 15½"
Private collection

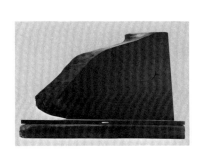

Pink Leaf, 1956
Wood painted black, 27½ x 46 x 7"
Museum of Art, Carnegie Institute,
Pittsburgh
Plate 10

Queen, 1956 (reconstructed 1979)
Wood painted black, 81 x 10 x 8"
Collection of the artist

Sky Totem, 1956
Wood painted black, 71 x 10½ x 12″
Sara Roby Foundation, New York

Undermarine Scape, 1956
Wood painted black, glass, and metal,
28½ x 17½ x 17″
Ben Mildwoff, New York
Plate 4

Black Wedding Cake, ca. 1957
Wood painted black, 38½″ high x 24″ diameter
Dorothy H. Rautbord, Palm Beach, Florida
Plate 5

The Bridge, 1957
Wood painted black, 5 x 96 x 5″
Private collection

Dark Shadows, 1957
Wood painted black, 72 x 9¾ x 4½″
The Newark Museum, New Jersey

Wedding Chest, 1957
Wood painted black, 16¼ x 21¾ x 15″
Frederic Mueller, New York

The Wave, 1958
Wood painted black, 28 x 21½ x 10½″
The Pace Gallery, New York
Plate 3.

MOON GARDEN + ONE

Sky Cathedral Presence, 1951–64
Wood painted black, 117 x 200 x 23"
Walker Art Center, Minneapolis;
gift of Mr. and Mrs. Kenneth N. Dayton
Plate 18

Sky Cathedral—Moon Garden Wall, 1956–59
Wood painted black, 85⅝ x 75¼ x 12⅛"
The Cleveland Museum of Art;
gift of the Mildred Andrews Fund
Plate 25

Black Mirror II, 1957
Wood painted black, 72 x 8¾ x 5¼"
Martha Jackson Gallery, Inc., New York
Plate 16

Bouquet (World Garden II), 1957
Wood painted black, 54 x 14 x 14"
Mark Le Jeune, Kapellenbos, Belgium
Plate 14

Moon Fountain, 1957
Wood painted black, 43 x 36½ x 34"
The Pace Gallery, New York
Plate 15

Moon Garden Reflections, ca. 1957
Wood painted black, 72 x 30 x 10"
Mr. and Mrs. Burton Tremaine,
Meriden, Connecticut
Plate 22

Sky Cathedral—Moon Garden + One,
1957–60
Wood painted black, 109 x 130 x 19"
Milly and Arnold Glimcher, New York
Plate 23

Tropical Garden II, 1957–59
Wood painted black, 71½ x 131¾ x 12"
Musée National d'Art Moderne,
Centre Georges Pompidou, Paris
Plate 20

*Night Landscape in
the Moon Garden,* 1958
Wood painted black, 72 x 9½ x 6½"
The Pace Gallery, New York

Sky Cathedral, 1958
Wood painted black, 102½ x 133½ x 20
Albright-Knox Art Gallery, Buffalo,
New York; George B. and
Jenny R. Mathews Fund, 1970
Plate 19

Sky Cathedral, 1958
Wood painted black, 135½ x 120¼ x 18"
The Museum of Modern Art, New York;
gift of Mr. and Mrs. Ben Mildwoff
Plate 24

Black Moon, 1959
Wood painted black, 81 x 30 x 18"
Martha Jackson Gallery, Inc., New York
Plate 26

Black Sun, 1959
Wood painted black, 30 x 24 x 10"
Mrs. H. Gates Lloyd, Haverford, Pennsylvania
Plate 27

Untitled, 1959
Wood painted black, 49 x 21¼ x 10½"
Private collection
Plate 17

Young Shadows, 1959–60
Wood painted black, 114 x 126 x 7¾"
Whitney Museum of American Art, New York;
gift of the Friends of the Whitney Museum
of American Art and Charles Simon
Plate 21

DAWN'S WEDDING FEAST

Dawn Cathedral Columns I and II,
1956–58
Wood painted white; two columns,
95½ x 6 x 6″ and 104 x 10 x 10″
Mr. and Mrs. Richard H. Solomon, New York

New Dawn Cathedral Column, 1956–58
Wood painted white, 109 x 12 x 12″
Mrs. Vivian Merrin, New York

Case with Five Balusters, 1959
Wood painted white, 28 x 63½ x 8″
Martha Jackson Gallery, Inc., New York
Plate 37

Dawn Lake, 1959
Wood painted white, 68¼ x 41½ x 4″
Martha Jackson Gallery, Inc., New York
Plate 36

Dawn Column I, 1959
Wood painted white, 92½ x 10½ x 10″
William A. Farnsworth Library and
Art Museum, Rockland, Maine
Plate 43

Dawn's Wedding Chapel I, 1959
Wood painted white, 90 x 51 x 6″
Dr. John W. Horton, Cupertino, California
Plate 28

Dawn's Wedding Chapel II, 1959
Wood painted white, 115⅞ x 83½ x 10½″
Whitney Museum of American Art, New York;
gift of the Howard and Jean Lipman
Foundation, Inc.
Plate 29

Dawn's Wedding Chapel IV, 1959–60
Wood painted white, 109 x 87 x 13½″
Philippe Braunschweig, La Chaux-de-Fonds,
Switzerland
Plate 44

Dawn's Wedding Chest, 1959
Wood painted white, 27 x 15 x 6″
Mr. and Mrs. Alvin S. Lane, New York
Plate 32

Dawn's Wedding Column, 1959
Wood painted white, 92 x 10 x 10″
Dr. John W. Horton, Cupertino, California

Dawn's Wedding Column, 1959
Wood painted white, 86 x 12 x 12″
William Louis-Dreyfus, New York

Dawn's Wedding Column, 1959
Wood painted white, 92½ x 14 x 12⅜″
Private collection
Plate 42

Dawn's Wedding Columns, 1959
Wood painted white; two columns,
72 x 4½ x 4½″ and 72 x 5 x 5″
Dorothy C. Miller, New York

Dawn's Wedding Columns (A and B), 1959
Wood painted white; two columns,
59 x 7 x 6″ and 60 x 7 x 7¼″
The Pace Gallery, New York
Plate 45

Dawn's Wedding Feast Columns, 1959
Wood painted white; two columns,
94 x 12 x 9″ and 94 x 17 x 9″
Menil Foundation, Houston
Plate 39

Dawn's Wedding Mirror, 1959
Wood painted white, 26½ x 31 x 7½″
Dr. John W. Horton, Cupertino, California
Plate 30

Dawn's Wedding Pillow, 1959
Wood painted white, 6½ x 36 x 13″
Dr. John W. Horton, Cupertino, California
Plate 33

Hanging Columns (from *Dawn's Wedding Feast*), 1959
Wood painted white; two columns, 72 x 6⅝" and 72 x 10⅛"
The Museum of Modern Art, New York; Blanchette Rockefeller Fund
Plate 40

Sun Disc, 1959
Wood painted white, 36 x 54 x 3"
Private collection
Plate 41

Totem II, 1959
Wood painted white, 110½ x 13½ x 14"
Martha Jackson Gallery, Inc., New York
Plate 38

America—Dawn, 1962–67
Wood painted white, 216 x 168 x 120"
The Art Institute of Chicago
Plate 46

THE ROYAL TIDES

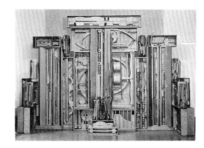

*An American Tribute to the
British People*, 1960–65
Wood painted gold, 122 x 171 x 42″
Trustees of the Tate Gallery, London
Plate 57

Royal Tide Dawn, 1960
Wood painted gold, 91 x 63 x 10⅝″
The Pace Gallery, New York
Plate 56

Royal Tide I, 1960
Wood painted gold, 96 x 40 x 8″
Howard and Jean Lipman, New York
Plate 53

Royal Tide II, 1960
Wood painted gold, 54 x 57 x 8″
Private collection
Plate 55

Royal Tide IV, 1960
Wood painted gold, 132 x 168 x 10″
Museum Ludwig, Cologne
Plate 49

Royal Winds I, 1960
Wood painted gold, 83 x 46 x 9½″
Mr. and Mrs. Kenneth S. Kaiserman,
Philadelphia
Plate 51

Half Moon I, 1961
Wood painted gold, 28 x 48 x 2″
Mr. and Mrs. Ulrich Franzen, New York

Half Moon II, 1961
Wood painted gold, 27⅝ x 48⅝ x 2½″
Center for the Performing Arts,
Smith College, Northampton, Massachusetts;
gift of the Class of 1967
Plate 50

Royal Tide II, 1961–63
Wood painted gold, 94½ x 126½ x 8″
Whitney Museum of American Art, New York;
gift of the artist
Plate 48

Sun Garden, Number I, 1964
Wood painted gold; three columns,
72 x 41 x 26″ overall
Mr. and Mrs. Charles M. Diker, New York
Plate 54

MRS. N'S PALACE

Mrs. N'S Palace, 1964–77
Wood painted black, black mirrored floor,
140 x 239 x 180″
The Pace Gallery, New York

PHOTOGRAPH CREDITS
Photographs of the works reproduced have been supplied, in many cases, by the owners or custodians of the works, as cited in the captions. Photographs have also been supplied by Archives of American Art; Galerie Daniel Gervis, Paris; Martha Jackson Gallery, Inc., New York; The Pace Gallery, New York. The following list applies to photographs for which an additional acknowledgment is due. Oliver Baker, Pls. 14, 27, pp. 82–83; Ferdinand Boesch, Pls. 12, 28, 54; Rudolph Burckhardt, Pls. 9, 17, 28, 30, 31, 32, 37, 47, 49, 52, 53, pp. 102–3, 108–9, 130–31, 190 (bottom row, center); Geoffrey Clements, Pls. 21, 29, Figs. 2, 3; Tom Crane, pp. 155–60, 166–67; D. James Dee, Fig. 13; Greenberg-May Productions, Inc., Pl. 19; Pedro E. Guerrero, pp. 32–49, Fig. 4; Helga Photo Studio, Inc., Pl. 41; Hickey-Robertson, Pl. 39; Scott Hyde, p. 182 (bottom row, left); Wendy Jeffers, p. 188 (middle row, center); Alix Jeffry, Fig. 1; Al Mozell, Pls. 15, 23, 56, pp. 164–65 (all pieces), 184 (middle left); Otto E. Nelson, Pls. 2, 16, 50, 51, p. 183 (bottom row, left); Fernand Perret, Pl. 44; Edward Peterson, Pl. 43; Eric Pollitzer, Pl. 25; George Roos, Fig. 10; Jeremiah W. Russell, Fig. 9, Pls. 6, 7, pp. 52–53, 58–59, 74–75, 80–81; John D. Schiff, Pls. 3, 11, 35, 38; Spadem, Paris (R.M.N.), Fig. 11; William Suttle, Pl. 45; Charles Uht, Pl. 42.

This book was published on the occasion of an exhibition at the Whitney Museum of American Art, New York, May 27–September 14, 1980.

The publication was organized at Clarkson N. Potter, Inc., by Carol Southern, Editor, assisted by Anne Goldstein, and at the Whitney Museum by Doris Palca, Head, Publications and Sales; Sheila Schwartz, Editor; James Leggio, Copy Editor; and Anne Munroe, Assistant.

The type was set by Fisher Composition on a Linotron 202 in a digitized form of Goudy Oldstyle, a face originally designed by Frederick Goudy about 1916 based on a typeface designed by Nicolas Jensen.

The book was printed by Sidney Rapoport in the Stonetone® process on 100 pound Lustro Offset Enamel dull supplied by the Lindenmeyer Paper Corporation and bound by A. Horowitz & Sons. Jackets and covers were separated and printed by Alithochrome Corporation.

The production of the book was supervised by Michael Fragnito and Teresa Nicholas.

The book was designed by BETTY BINNS GRAPHICS/Betty Binns and Abby Goldstein.